Apostasy Devotional

Apostasy Devotional - A Daily Guide Exposing False Shepherds

Copyright by James Russell 2009, 2011. All Rights Reserved

Published by: James Russell Publishing.com

Author: James Russell / Edited by: Carole Marie

Printed and bound in USA

,,,,,,

ISBN-10: 0-916367-62-2

I0278553

ISBN-13: 978-0-916367-62-6

Category: Christianity/Fundamentalism

No portion of this publication may be reproduced, stored in a retrieval system, or transmitted in any form by any means, except brief quotations in printed reviews, without prior permission of the publisher.

A Gift For:
_____
From:
_____

DEDICATION

To the Lord of Lord's
&
King of Kings - Jesus of Nazareth

FORWARD

This daily devotional will bring you back into the true church of Jesus Christ of Nazareth. Be aware you have already fallen victim to the global apostate church system as you will soon find out. You are about to be set free, just like our good shepherd said you would... if you have ears to hear- John 10:1,14. Let's now unshackle the binding chains. You will also learn some tips on witnessing to the lost... easy things you can do!

What does the word apostate mean? It means defector, deserter, traitor, backslider, heretic. Judas was an apostate. He pretended to be a Christian. Most churchgoing Christians today are seriously apostate and do not even know it! Their pastors have deceived them so badly the apostate church appears legitimate. If you feel like you are being scolded, you are right. This writing is a warning to awaken you and to set you free from apostate bondage. That is good news for you!

This book will destroy your faith! The Bible says you don't need a pastor to get to heaven! 1 Tim. 2:5. If you do not obey (by doing) Jesus' commands, you are a liar and all liars go into the lake of fire - 1 John 2:4. Satan has ministers teaching you - 2 Cor 11:15. Yes, you! You think antichrist means those who act evil, but anyone who replaces Jesus Christ or his true gospel with a distorted or changed gospel is antichrist and that's what pastors do today. Remember that word, substitution! It is the great key to apostasy.

The purpose of this text is to make you question, think and respond to contending for the faith once delivered to the saints. We must speak out and defend the faith. Why? - Because God says to. To save those who are deceived and to take back our gospel from lazy, uncaring apostate pastors who have hijacked the gospel concealing the good news from the eyes of the public... and to go forth and proclaim the gospel to the lost. The one thing Christians totally fail to do with their pastor's full blessing.

You are going to learn a lot here. You will soon be enabled with knowledge to detect the serpents masquerading as angels.

Apostasy Devotional

WHY THIS NEEDS TO BE WRITTEN

Pastors are getting away with apostate ministries and too few church members are speaking out to expose the great falling away from Biblical teaching (doctrine). As a result, church members think they are saved when in fact they are not saved and heading straight to hell.

We must absolutely place 100% of the blame on those who are corrupting the gospel... the pastors. They are the leaders and they are the teachers and they are the wolves disguised as trustworthy servants of the Lord. You can't blame the sheep when a false shepherd pastor is to blame. The pastor gets the heat.

You may find it hard to believe that millions of pastors are imposters, fakes, liars and deceivers working for Satan. I sure did, once upon a time. That all changed when I discovered these holier-than-thou pastors could care less to go and save the lost. They won't go seek those who are lost as Jesus did. They will only put an advertisement in a newspaper to invite the worst of the worst evil sinners and then let these unrepentant sinners prey on the congregation. The wolf just opened the gate so predators may enter to devour the flock. Amazing, but true!

Churchgoers are sitting next to unrepentant and unsaved child-molesting homosexual monsters like murderers, rapists, gang thugs, thieves, adulterers, etc., with the "ignorant and incompetent" pastor's full blessing. The early church never permitted such abominations to associate fellowship with these unrepentant devils. Today, going to church can be inviting yourself to demonic attack, thanks to your pastor who is operating a for-profit enterprise under the guise of a church of God and further using a non-profit enterprise as a cover up to evade paying taxes, etc. God would not defile himself to enter such a place! Don't kid yourself, God is still holy.

You will learn a lot in these pages, if you have ears to hear. If you are willing to read the Word of God and obey it, not trample His word under your feet as the pastors do today.

You also will have a new responsibility, to expose apostasy when you see it. The lost is in your church and the church next door and...!

WHY I HAD TO WRITE YOU

I am writing what few dare to write, the truth that needs to be told. Yes, a few have written books on apostasy, but only a handful has. There are many more highly educated and qualified faithful servants of the Lord writing powerful newsletters, magazines, radio and Internet forums to expose apostasy and may God bless each and all of them! God needs more workers for the harvest. He is hiring. Will you apply and accept employment?

Tens of thousands of pastors, whom are vastly more qualified than I, remain silent! I wished not to write of apostasy and delayed it for as long as I could, but like a burning flame within, I can be silent no more... souls depend on it! Contending for the faith, one delivered to the saints was not my idea of ministry, but now I realize it is the ministry of all true disciples of Christ... all of us. Silence is not golden; it is outright rebellion against God! If a few can be saved then let God be given the glory!

CAN APOSTATES BE SAVED?

The Bible gives us an example to warn those who are being deceived or are about to be deceived. However, the Bible says that apostates are already damned and cursed. There is no clear command to try to save apostate believers, only to warn of their tactics and ways so others will not be deceived. That is the purpose of this writing. Jesus sternly warned, *"Do not be deceived."* Once you do you are doomed, unless by God's mercy. You open your eyes so you can see and be saved. Not reading an accurate Bible and blindly believing pastor sermons will deceive you with amazing precision and effectiveness! And the process can be painful. Paul Proctor, an Internet Christian Writer explains, *"One cannot be the salt of the earth without occasionally stinging the open sores of sin."*

A BIBLICAL COMMAND

The Bible commands believers to contend for the faith once delivered to the saints. And amazingly, pastors conveniently leave out that (and other) commands from any of their sermons! Isn't it time you obey the Lord your God and dare to disobey your pastor? Yes! It is time!

A DAILY DEVOTIONAL

Each day of the year you will be given a "thought to ponder" and through this process your eyes will be opened as to seeing that certainly something is wrong with what you are experiencing in your church.

You will begin to see the errors, but most of all the, "omissions" taking place that pastors use to deceive their flock in Jesus' name. It's not always what is being preached, but what is not being preached and not being taught is the great secret of the apostate church system.

YOU WILL BE SHOCKED

At first you will be defensive and appalled at what you read here, but please go directly to your Bible, the Holy Scriptures, and verify that what is being said here is actually in harmony with God's Word. Oh, yes. You will be shocked! But remember, even Jesus said that the end times falling away will be so great that even he proclaims there would be few found to have faith on the earth. The faith he was talking about is true Biblical faith. What we have in our churches today is a "counterfeit Christianity" that sounds Christian and sound Biblical, but is serving a "different God" and a "different Jesus" than mentioned in the Bible. Amazingly intelligent Satan is to have pulled this off with so much ease. You will learn just how smart Satan truly is.

FIRST BOOK EVER WRITTEN

Nobody (except the Bible) has ever written and published a daily devotional that specifically exposes apostasy. This is the first! The Christian devotionals you find in the bookstores and libraries will smother you with highly selective Biblical verses that only "say nice things" just like pastor sermons do. Nothing critical or bad is ever being exposed as it would "upset" the mood of the reader. The Bible upsets the mood of the reader! It proclaims the good and the bad, not just juicy tidbits to elevate the ecstasy of the reader. The Word of God is balanced and this is your first lesson in apostasy training, the Bible is being manipulated by pastors and famous Christian authors picking and choosing verses out of context to create a "new doctrine" a "new faith" a "new gospel" with a "new Jesus" and even a "brand new Bible" and millions of people are being hoodwinked and fooled.

HOW TO READ THIS BOOK

It is okay to read the entire book in one sitting or to read many pages per day. I know that I would, being curious as to what knowledge is coming on the next paragraph. But when you finish the book, then use it as it was designed, to read one paragraph entry per day for the entire year. There is much knowledge within these pages and it will take a long time for it to all sink in, so don't be surprised to discover you will be using it for many years to come!

RESTRAIN YOUR ANGER

When you discover you have been fooled by your pastor you will become angry at the entire apostate system and those who have fooled you. What you should do is what I have done to manage this natural anger and that is to channel this energy into taking corrective action to expose them, just as the Bible instructs us to do... expose them to shame and ridicule for their lies and deception by contending for the faith once delivered to the saints! I know how angry you will get knowing these pastors are going about lying, stealing and deceiving innocent people and even these innocent people will doubt and disbelieve you, choosing to side with their pastor, church, denomination, etc. Just remember, they are rejecting the true Word of God's Bible, not you alone. They prefer to believe a lie than to believe the truth that will set them free. So, don't take rejection personal, just obey the Lord and contend for the faith and keep learning about the great apostasy. There's a lot you can do. You can write gospel tracts to expose these lying pastors. You can even write a book! How about a Web site or blog page? Even little business cards can be made as flyers exposing apostate churches. What is important is to get involved to save the lost and to remember that most all churchgoers are not saved.

WHO IS FOOLING WHO?

We are all being duped by our pastors and the pastors are duping each other and we are all falling into the pit. This is serious business as heaven bound Christians are actually heading to Hell and they are being fooled into believing they are saved, but they are not saved! We need to wake up and obey the Lord before it is too late. Too many of us are listening to and obeying our pastors. Keep an open mind when you read this book and your Bible. Dare to follow the Lord. Be strong to give up your religion to follow Him. Your eternal destiny lies in His hands, not your pastor's! Find out who you are really serving... it's going to surprise you. Let's get started.

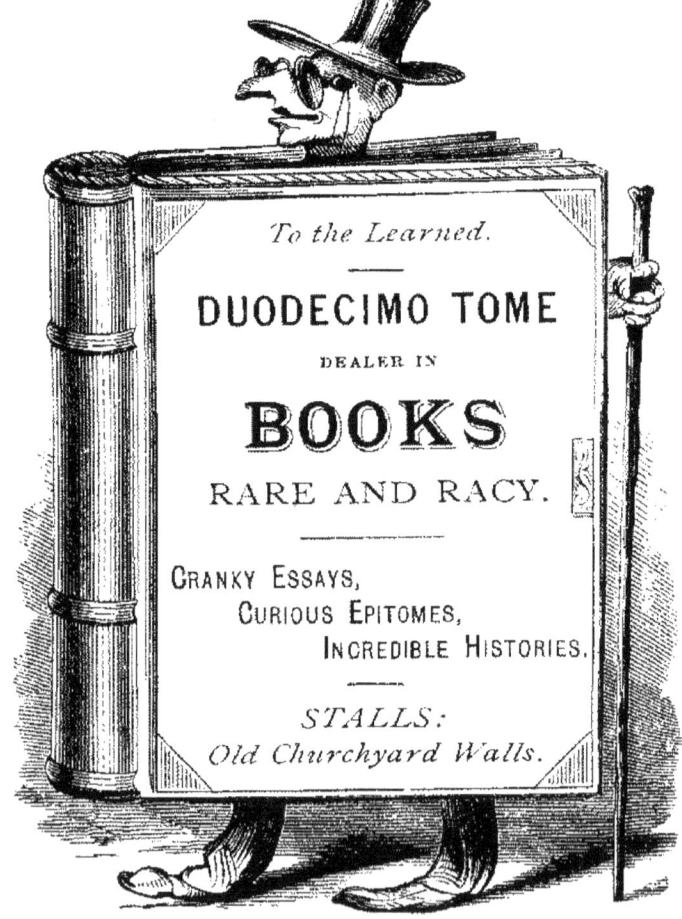

WORKING FOR GOD

Your pastor will teach you that working for God is working for his church. But he won't teach you that bearing good fruit is actually going out and saving the lost, obeying Jesus of Nazareth's command to do so.

Working for the pastor's church is not working for God and it is not a Christian practice according to the Bible. It's just another fabrication by pastors to continue to control the brethren and get them to serve himself, not the Lord.

Be wary of working for the church!

CHAPTER 1

Most Everything preached from the pulpit today is puffery mixed with Biblical passages and this book is going to expose these pastors and in doing so, will set you free to serve the Lord directly. Get ready for a rough and ready journey and the ride of your life!

January 1.

1 Corinthians 11:2 Paul gave thanks for holding on to the teachings, just as he passed them on. Imagine there were pastors already perverting the gospel as he spoke. Today, pastors are having a field day changing the Word of God with nobody to stop them and none too few to expose them. Perhaps you may bear good fruit sounding the alarm of warning to those being deceived. It is the least you could do. It is wrong to remain silent. Do something!

January 2.

If you are not standing up for what is right, you're wrong. Are you telling people (other than churchgoers) the gospel? How is it that your pastor is not teaching you how? A false shepherd will never teach, preach or instruct the flock how to proclaim the gospel to the lost. Cults will! Even the Great Commission is now horrific all perverted by the Great Apostate Church System. The falling away is complete when silent Christians do not care to share the gospel to the lost. It's that bad!

January 3.

"You shall be witnesses to me..."
Christians who are not witnessing for Christ are not obeying him. The Bible never delegated this command to pastors exclusively; it is for every Christian to obey. What have you done to personally share the gospel to the lost yesterday, last week, and last month. What are you doing to:
Reach homosexuals.
Reach Mormons.
Reach Roman Catholics.
Reach Jehovah Witnesses.
Reach the homeless.
Reach the poor.
Reach our troubled youth.
Reach the elderly.
Reach prostitutes.
Reach drug users.
Reach the lost for Christ.

Just who are you reaching out to share the gift of eternal life? Why is your pastor not teaching you how? If church is just to listen to a pastor's talking sermons, then you will end up a do-nothing Christian that will be cut off the vine. Jesus promises you it will be so. Go share the gospel. That is your job! But it's not on your pastor's mind. That's why he does not stress this command in his sermons. He does not want competition. If you start your own ministry then he can't tap you for money to support his ministry. That's why pastors don't like to preach personal evangelism responsibility. It's a subject they rather ignore and they do a good job of it too.

January 4.

Only you can reach the lost within the circle of your life. Do not delay. It will be too late when you stand near their casket to tell them you are sorry. Tell them the Good News of the gospel of Jesus Christ. If you can, send them a gift with a gospel tract and do it today. Tomorrow may be way too late.

January 5.

Many professing Christians go to church for years and never learn the importance of proclaiming the gospel to the lost. They do not care to share the gospel. They are cold, not even luke warm. Nobody cares that the lost are going to hell, as long as it is not them. This is not the way. It is not what God's Word says to do. It is the path to hell's eternal fire. Beware! You must be born again to enter heaven.

January 6.

Isn't it odd that religious cults aggressively proclaim their false gospel to the lost, but Christians don't? Jesus told us to share his gospel and pastors refuse to comply. They will not even demand that their flock obey the Master's command. They have become false shepherds. Are you following one?

January 7.

Ask yourself when was the last time you heard your pastor preach a sermon (or a sermon series) on how to share the gospel to the lost? Likely, it's never or rarely. This is clear and convincing proof your pastor is taking you down a different path than what Jesus and the apostles taught.

January 8.

No matter how sweet and loving your pastor appears, you must judge him by his true fruits. Not by his lovingly sweet sermons, but how many of the lost are being saved and that doesn't mean church membership.

January 9.

Did you know the Bible gives no authorization to pastors to be performing marriages? Think for a moment that Jesus and not one Apostle performed a marriage vow ceremony or even spoke of it to be performed by pastors. Today, pastors make you believe they have the power and authority to perform marriage. Now how come you never thought of this? That is because pastors are very good at hiding truth from your eyes.

January 10.

Did your pastor ever tell you what shirt to wear? Well, he should have done so many years ago. You see many Christians wearing the devil's clothing, especially T-shirts. You are thinking of those evil looking styles, but I am thinking of the ones you wear, like the shirt with no pocket. Satan loves those shirts because you can't put any gospel literature, tracts or Christian gifts to give to people you meet or leave here and there in your daily travels. Think about why your pastor refuses to offer you advice on how to witness and share the gospel.

January 11.

A Christian is to avoid sin at all cost. Your pastor has failed to tell you that it is not a sin to share the gospel to the lost. You see if you look around in your church you will find nobody bragging about how many souls they have reached for Jesus last week. This is sin. Your pastor is actually causing you to disobey the Lord's command to share the gospel when he fails to teach and instruct you truth as it was given to the saints.

January 12.

Obey Jesus... disobey your pastor! It is time for you to stop listening to the sweet honeysuckle sermons your pastor is singing you and start aligning yourself to obeying the commands of Jesus. Example: Go share the gospel, bear good fruit, etc. Who are you really obeying and following?

January 13.

Do you believe your pastor is a good shepherd?
Most Christians answer, "Yes." They deny Jesus and call him a liar. Jesus said, *"I am the good shepherd."* He also said, *"Follow me."*

January 14.

Any hypnotist can tell you that pastors are using hypnotic devices to get you to believe and obey him. This is one of the bewitching powers given to pastors by Satan. Watch out for any pastor telling you what to say or when to sit down or when to applaud or when to praise God. These are "reinforcing" tactics to control your mind into deeper states of hypnosis. Television ministers do it too. This hypnosis is real and your pastor is using it upon you despite your disbelief.

January 15.

What is your pivot point? You need to be able to identify the precise moment you were born again, the moment when your life changed.

January 16.

What is your foundation? This is important because for many Christians their church is, when it should be the Word of God as written in the Bible. Jesus is the Word and that is why your foundation must be on the solid rock of the Word of God. Do you obey the Bible? You will need to read it to find out.

January 17.

Beware of counterfeit Bibles. You must read the King James Version (KJV) as other versions are seriously flawed with horrific errors of interpretation. Has your pastor informed you of these corrupt versions? If not, find out why he is so silent and not warning others.

January 18.

Follow me. That is what Jesus said. The apostles were all devout Jews and they had to make a choice; follow Jesus or Judaism. You also must make the same choice. Follow Jesus or your church/pastor. Which will it be? You can't serve two masters. You will love one and despise the other.

January 19.

Do not follow the counsel of the ungodly (Jer 15:16), even if the counsel is a pastor as he can be an apostate leading you to destruction under the guise of holiness. Apostasy comes from pastors, those who lead a flock. So you have been warned.

January 20.

Jer 15:16. Look it up. Did you read, *The Lost Gospel of John*?

January 21

Proverbs 16:6 says ... *"and by the fear of the Lord men depart from evil."* Evil can be the very church Christians attend, full of apostate members disobeying God's Word, yet they will not leave for their pastor has taught them not to fear the Lord....a perfect ingredient for disaster.

WHO'S DREAM?

Your pastor is full of wants, needs and desires, but it is his dreams that are the most dangerous of all. His dreams fly counter to the dreams of God. His dreams oppose the desires of Jesus of Nazareth. His dreams exalts his will, not God's will. Reading your Bible will show this is true.

If you participate in your pastor's dreams to build a bigger church building you are in full agreement with your pastor and you have now become the enemy of God. The Lord does not desire large church buildings. He does not desire church temples. He desires the lost to be saved.

But as you can see, your pastor's dreams are not what God dreams and is now not what you dream! You have become a partnership with your pastor to build something God does not want built. Your allegiance is now compromised because you listen to your pastor and not your Lord.

Is this what you really want? To oppose God?

BLASPHEMY

What is blasphemy? Well, you know what it is. It is saying things that insult God. It's also your pastor's sermons. Preaching things that insult the Lord is blasphemy. Especially, preaching things the Lord never said or meant, taking His Word out of context and failing to preach a true gospel. Even failing to preach the whole counsel of God is blasphemy. This is a subtle blasphemy, the new blasphemy, the modern day blasphemy taking place in the church pulpits today.

Are you guilty of blasphemy? You are if you are a member of that church doing it. You are a willing participant if you finance and support that pastor.

What you read in this book appears, at first, to be blasphemous, but what is written here is the truth and it is backed up by the Bible. You may not like the truth because the truth causes pain. Jesus caused a lot of pain as he spoke the truth. Of course, the truth is painful to a lie. Do you welcome truth or do you prefer your pastor's lies? Who will you choose this day?

January 22

Jesus had great compassion to the people and felt sorry for them as sheep without a shepherd. But he scolded, insulted and had scathing words to the leaders deceiving the flock. So it is today that God's servants contending for the faith must not play footsie-footsie with pastors misleading and deceiving the flock. When will you shout down these apostate pastors when they are preaching falsely? When?

January 23

Blasphemy is accepted in church today. You will hear pastors preaching and using the name of Jesus (or God's name) in vain. They do this as an expression of speech, but it is still blasphemy. Do not think Satan is not inside your church... he's right before your eyes in the perceived holy place speaking lies in God's name. This is nothing new. The Pharisees did it too!

If you can't hear a pastor lie in the first three to five minutes into his sermon, you need ears to hear! Sometimes they don't lie every once in awhile to throw you off tract if you dare suspect them, but this honesty is actually a very rare event. Pastors lie even when holding the Bible in hand saying, *"I preach the Word of God."* They preach about things God cares not of. They preach not to save the lost. They preach not Jesus' commands. They preach not Jesus' warnings. They preach not how to witness. They preach not how to distribute gospel tracts. They preach not how to Glorify God. They preach not the whole counsel of truth. They preach not ... You got the idea. They leave out the true gospel and that is called preaching lies! And when he finishes his sermon nobody cares to preach or share the gospel to the lost. <u>Remember this</u>!

January 24

Do not think you will escape God's wrath because you give money to your church to publish a magazine to save the lost. That is not Biblical. *You* are to be a light. *You* are the salt. *You* must be personally involved witnessing to the lost. *You* are to have your own ministry and *you* are the royal priesthood. *You* keep on refusing to share the gospel to strangers, sinners and the poor beggars *you* see every day! *You* ignore them. How dare you disobey the Lord! Be ashamed, repent and go save the lost without your lazy false pastor's blessing. Turn from *your* evil ways!

January 25

Substitution is the greatest tool created by Satan for implantation by apostate pastors ever devised to fool men. It was used in the Garden of Eden. Remember this word as it will unlock the mystery of iniquity. *"Substitution is the mystery of iniquity exposed!"* More will be explained later.

January 26

It is fair to blame pastors for the sad state of the church. Why? Because they rule! Many even own the deed to the church. They are the leaders whom the flock follows. Wherever there is apostasy you will find a smiling, jolly pastor deceiving the people. In the most perverse cults you find a pastor running the show.

January 27

Which day is the Sabbath? It's not Sunday according to the Bible. Are you curious? Read Acts 13:14, 27, 42, 44, 15:19, 17:2, 18:4, 11, 19:8 and 10. Surprised? Pastors have been fooling millions of Christians and getting away with it for so long they have turned wrong, right. But God still demands obedience to his Word no matter what your pastor says otherwise. So, who are you really obeying, your pastor or your Lord?

January 28

The moment compromise is accepted into a church and upheld by a pastor, the church is now apostate. You must voice your concern and warning. If they do not repent you are to leave the church. If unrepentant homosexuals invade your church and they are allowed to stay then get out. Follow and obey the Lord, not your church.

January 29

Place a small piece of paper in your pocket. Now take it out and place it somewhere and walk away. That's how easy it is to distribute a gospel tract to reach the lost for your Master. Doing nothing is working for your other master who does not want you to share the gospel. Which master are you really serving? Master Jesus or Master Pastor?

January 30

Now here's something your pastor will not preach, *"If you do not gather you scatter."* Jesus taught this, but your pastor feels it is not necessary or worthy to preach about it. List how many sermons relate to you witnessing to the lost. Go ahead and do this so you can prove to yourself your pastor truly is concealing critical components of the Bible.

January 31

What is God's will for you? Listen to all the sermons your pastor feeds you about God's will for you and you will not hear...*"Go ye into all the world and preach the gospel to every creature."* Mark 16:15. Today you must consider your ways and obey the Lord, not your pastor! Get your gospel tracts and begin sharing the gospel to the lost. That is God's will to have your own outreach ministry, not to be an apostate church member.

One Month Has Passed. Eleven More to Go!

Yes, you have learned a lot last month, but hold on to your seat! There is much more shocking truths yet to come. Remember, our Lord Jesus and his apostles all gave us clear warnings of apostasy and false shepherds.

It is depressing to read, but absolutely essential to know truth and to be wise as serpents as Jesus commanded.

Every Christian must study apostasy, so a lack of knowledge will not cause you and others to perish.

CHAPTER 2

The moment you believe you are in the right church WATCH OUT! Millions of people are in cult churches and wholeheartedly believe with great faith they are in a true Bible believing church, but they are not. The deception is extremely powerful and fools even the most educated beings on planet earth with great ease. Unless you have "studied" apostate churches you are in GREAT DANGER! Most Christians will ignore warnings.

DID YOU KNOW?

Believe it or Not! **It is True!**

YOUR PASTOR
Signed a docmument* promising he would...

NEVER expose or warn you of a false teaching or unfaithful undersheperd is preaching a false gospel.

NEVER preach a sermon condemning sodomites or declare they will never be members of his church.

NEVER expose or renounce other religious beliefs that are apostate and unbiblical.

NEVER declare his church is controlled by Jesus Christ and Him alone and there is no other authority.

NEVER preach politically incorrect sermons of any or all apostasies infiltrating true Christianity.

NEVER preach subjects in the Bible that God hates; idolatry, homosexuals, false shepherds, lying church denominations. He won't preach the entire Gospel.

NEVER tell us who to vote for that will benefit the church or society or endorse a candidate to oppose an anti-Christian candidate.

NEVER expose abortion clinics in your town by telling the name of the doctors or lead a protest.

*(Internal Revenue Service: Church Tax Guide)   **Over...** ➤

This is Really Happening in <u>Your</u> Church!

Apostasy Devotional

YOUR PASTOR
Will not preach the true Gospel of Jesus

"The Truth Will Set You Free" - Jesus of Nazareth
(continued from other side)

He Will Not Cry Out Warnings
NEVER voice opposition of politicians enacting laws that will harm Christians. He can't be a watchman!

He Will Not Preach the Entire Gospel
NEVER tell the congregation anti-Christ regulations is sensoring the sermons and preaching of the pastor. And the government tells the pastor what he can or cannot preach in the pulpit. Sermons are secretly censured.

The Great Falling Away is Here
NEVER tell you the government owns the church via incorporation laws and if certain sermons are preached the church will be confiscated and church members put in prison! Secrets your pastor hides from you!

He is a Government Spy
NEVER reveal the pastor is reporting church members names, donations, time and other private matters to the government. Yes he is! He must, by law!

He is a Dangerous Hireling
NEVER let on that the pastor is a hireling of the state, that he is an "officer" of the state, doing state business.

Government Tells Him What to Preach
NEVER tell the congregation the state controls the church, the pastor and the doctrines of the church.

Suppress the True & Complete Gospel
NEVER reveal pastor, bishop, elders and deacons are "trustees" subject to these incorporation laws that will prevent them from preaching certain Bible teachings.

Your Church is a Government Church
NEVER disclose the church belongs to the pastor and held in "trust" to the state. Government owned church!

He Works For Ceasar Not God
NEVER refrain from telling all church members each April they must pay taxes to the state. A pastor must do do this or he will lose his church. But he pays no taxes.

He Will Only Say Nice Things!
NEVER expose the licensing of cult churches planned for your city or renounce pornography establishments, un-biblical school teaching, sinful events, etc., in your community. The pastor must remain silent and not warn you of the danger. He has betrayed his trust and Lord.

© *LEARN MORE! VISIT:* **JamesRussellPublishing.com**

This is another topic too deep for us here, but it is critical you know that your pastor and denomination has forsaken Jesus when he incorporated his church. You need to understand that the state now has taken over the church and even forbids what the pastor can preach, say or do. He can't preach or teach against other religions, homosexuals, political persons and much more!

Creating an incorporate church and constructing a church building creates a government partnership. The pastor is now serving two masters and obeys the government more than he obeys the Lord. Did you know the trickery is that "elders" and "deacons" are nothing but hireling smokescreens, as they are "corporate trustee" identities? All this to obtain a tax-exempt status! None of this is Biblical.

Again, the New Testament church never built any church structure and pastors did not "rule" the church nor get paid for their services and they never embraced Rome or any Government as a "partnership in the church." You should study this subject, so you can see how apostate churches function and deceive. You could write a book on this!

The gospel tract above on the preceding pages is my attempt to expose these pastors who have signed away their trust, betraying their Lord and their congregation for the almighty dollar. And what is frightening, almost all the pastors have done so! And those who have not, are likely hirelings for a denomination that has on a corporate administration level.

The only pastor that would not sign such a document? He would not own or operate a church building or be a tax-exempt, non-profit entity. But how would you know if he is or is not? You will have to check out the state, county, city or federal government records to discover the truth. If he is taking money from the congregation, he has likely signed that dreaded government document and agreed to not preach the entire gospel. Beware of these pastors. They are everywhere!

What to do? You should be meeting in homes, not in church buildings or other buildings where pastors are running and controlling everything. The Bible never authorizes pastors to be leaders over the flock. Go ahead, read your Bible. Its not there! Can you see now just how so many people are being fooled? Do not come under the subjection of any pastor!

February 1

When you distribute gospel tracts you are putting the kingdom of God first. Then all other things will be given to you. Today apostate churches are full of beggars pleading God for favors, yet these religious fakers have no mercy on the lost. They pray, *"Lord, deliver me, but I will not share the gospel. I will not obey your Son's word."* Are you asking in vain? Amiss? When will you wake up and follow the Lord? When?

February 2

When you begin to pass out gospel tracts, your Christian buddies at church will not support you. Your pastor will inwardly frown, smile visibly, but he will not support you. They will not give you financial support as was done in Acts. Be prepared to discover your good church has gone bad long ago. It is only now you are beginning to see the church has a form of Godliness and no desire to even save the lost in its own neighborhood. It is the farthest thought from the mind and actually avoided.

February 3

Colossians 4:2 *"Devote yourself to prayer, being watchful and thankful."* Be watchful for what? A wolf in sheep's clothing! To be on your guard to detect deceiving pastors. Remember this, those who are deceived do not know it. You will find the truth by reading the Bible (KJV).

February 4

Read the Bible and you see prophets, Jesus, apostles all giving warnings not to follow liars and they demand obedience to God's written Word. Compare sermons given by pastors today and it follows a different theme... a different gospel and even a different Jesus.

February 5

1 Corinthians 16:13 says, *"Be on guard, stand firm in the faith; be men of courage; be strong. Do everything in love."* Pastors preach the love portion with great ease and to be strong in attending his church, but the rest is given silence. To contend for the faith will expose apostasy and that is why pastors are keeping silent. A wolf will not warn sheep before the

kill, it is against his nature.

February 6

Anything is acceptable in the church today. Speakers may speak lies. Pastors can blaspheme, teach a false gospel and the congregation applauds and cheers. It can't happen in your church? It likely is and you don't know it because you don't understand, read or obey the Bible. That's how the church deceives. It is an abomination of desolation in God's eyes.

February 7

Pastors teach that church is for sinners. It is not and never has been. No Apostle ever let sinners into fellowship meetings. Some pastors did and the apostles became infuriated and discipline was enacted to purge the sinners out. Today pastors advertise anyone to come to their worship service, even rapists, murderers, homosexuals, child molesters and thieves. They need to be saved first, not admitted into the presence of the flock. The wolf is the enemy of the sheep and will open the gate to let predators in. Think about that. Who is really sitting beside or behind you? Bile says to purge those unrepentant sinners out of the church. 1 Cor. 5-7.

February 8

Would you dare to obey the Lord to expose false pastors and other wrongdoings in the church today? If not you, then who will? You see, God wants us all to stand firm in the faith and share the true gospel. Your silence is wrongdoing. You must speak up or your silence is denying Jesus even inside your own church. Contend for the faith!

February 9

Your pastor's church is not the house of the Lord! It never was and never will be. It will remain the pastor's kingdom which is not Biblical. The Bible never authorized the building of any physical church. The Apostle Paul was the greatest church builder and he never built a brick and mortar church. The saints met in homes in small numbers and no pastor "owned" the deed to a church to obtain personal wealth by collecting money from the saints. Read the Bible. It exposes apostasy.

February 10

Which version of the Bible is your pastor using? You need to know. Why? Because the NKJV omits the word Lord 66 times, the word God 51 times, the word heaven 50 times, the word repent 44 times, the word blood 23 times, the word Jehovah entirely and amazingly the word hell 22 times. No wonder the flock is misled when pastors use word-omitting Bibles. What version are you using? You can't obey the Lord if you don't have his Word for instruction, the King James Version of the Bible.

February 11

When you see the population in society full of tattoos, body mutilating piercing and cussing you can blame yourself for doing nothing to correct the problem. Your pastor is not helpful to teach you how to save the lost. Due to silent Christians, the pagans multiply not knowing the way to salvation. It is late, but you can repent and begin your ministry today. Do not do what your pastor does, which is nothing to save the lost.

February 12

The sealed environment is controlled by the pastor. Close the doors and speak powerful sermons the lost can not hear and never will hear. Bold, courageous speakers preach wonderful sermons and testimonies, yet these same apostate churchgoing wannabe leaders will not preach the gospel to the unsaved. You never see them working for the Lord. Go downtown. Where are all the servants of the Lord? They can not be found. Jesus said that you will know them by their fruit.

February 13

Worship services. We see churches advertising in newspapers and billboards, but the apostles never advertised. They fellowshipped and ate meals together in homes by strict <u>exclusive invitation only</u>, but the formal structure we see inside churches today are *not* Biblical. Worshipping the Lord is to obey Him and do what pleases Him. Not once did Jesus command pastors to conduct worship services or build church buildings. Pastors are *not* obeying the Bible. They have found a way to *sell* worship services for profit. The apostasy is worse than you think.

MORE SERMONS NEEDED

There is a relentless bombardment of sermons being hurled upon believers assaulting them without mercy. But you will find that many sermons are mysteriously missing. You won't hear pastors preaching on "certain subjects" that may offend people or cause their feelings to be hurt.

As if Jesus walked this earth appeasing everyone he met and preaching no hard thing. That is what your pastor is teaching you and to become like Jesus, the Jesus he manufactured, to say no harmful thing to anyone. Be at peace!

So, let us go on being a loving Christian and say to all, *"God Speed and God Bless You"* while the wrath of God remains on them and they are headed straight to eternal damnation. That's the sort of Christian your pastor wants you to be. Don't call people sinners! Don't make waves. Be amiable and let the damned remain lost in their sin.

It's all part of the pastor's sermon scheme!

OUR GOD HATES NOTHING

The God you serve, the loving God that hates nothing is not the God of the Bible. He is a fictitious God your pastor has fabricated to feed you a false gospel.

The God of the Bible has a hatred for sin, homosexuals, liars, thieves, murderers, pride, greed and the list goes on. Of course, you knew that, didn't you? But how come your pastor does not preach on these subjects? How come Christians are so silent on these issues?

The newspapers are full of evil and bad news, but little do pastors care to reach out to the lost in these neighborhoods to save the sinners causing all this misery and grief. Pastors like to hide in their churches and preach bold sermons, but crime and sin and horror is left to continue.

Jesus walked the streets preaching, but that's what no pastor will do and it's exactly what he wants you to do too, to become like him, a faithful do-nothing churchgoer!

February 14

Playing church. Things are going on inside churches that are nothing but entertainment. Even pastor sermons are full of lies. They preach up a storm to dazzle the flock, but they will inherit an eternal whirlwind of grief. Corruption in the church is so perverse it appears legitimate and is accepted as perfectly normal, but it is an insult to God to play church and to disobey His commands. They worship in vain. Obey the Lord, not your church and not your pastor. Loyalty is to the Lord and Him alone.

February 15

Gospel for sale! Pastors sell the gospel. They build churches and sell their sermons by charging a "collection fee" but that is not enough. They create sermons to be sold for personal enrichment. They market the products to Christians which is not Biblical whatsoever.

February 16

How much money has the rich pastor given to you? Nothing! He is supposed to share the money not take it all for himself. A collection of money is to send forth an evangelist to save the lost and to be shared with the saints. Today pastors just take, keep, hoard and send no evangelists into their own communities and certainly do not give money back to their congregation. The money follows a one-way street right into a dead-end; the pastor's pocket. This activity is not Biblical.

February 17

Preach the blood of Christ and him crucified. That is the gospel. It is not pleasant. In fact, it is offensive and foolishness to those who are perishing, but it is the salvation of God. It is his plan of salvation, not ours or anyone else message. We must not change the gospel, sweeten it or leave out the core message of the gospel. Jesus died, shed his blood on that cross for the remission of our sins. That's the way it is. But notice how pastors do their best to avoid this subject. They rather preach other things each week on Sunday. What did your pastor preach about last week?

February 18

Church attendance is better than sharing the gospel. Do you really believe your pastor believes and encourages this? He does! Church attendance is at the deep core of his heart. He is not concerned with what is at the deep core of God's heart. Jesus came to save the lost, not to create pastoral kingdoms. He did not come to perfect church attendance. He did not come to build physical church buildings and He did not tell us to attend church services performed by pastors. Christians would be better served by meeting in homes in small groups as the early church did. Now all may speak, share, teach and "fellowship" and urge each other to share the gospel and most important to let Christ run his church.

February 19

What about foreign missions? How about preaching right here in our own towns, cities, and communities? You can't find one church going Christian near a courthouse where the lost need to hear the gospel. Go see for yourself. Pastors have totally abandoned the Great Commission. Even the big rich pastors won't be caught preaching nearby.

February 20

Pastoral power. There is no such thing in the Bible. There is no example of any "pastor" having special powers or gifts. Think about that! Evangelists did reveal power as they share the gospel to reach the lost, as the early church apostles and disciples so demonstrated, but no pastor was given such authority. Two-thousand years later we see pastors now have all the "perceived" power, status, focus, control, leadership, sermons, etc. None of it is Biblical whatsoever. Pastors get up on their privately owned stage and play to entertain the flock as if they were special, chosen, powerful servants of God. Many are empowered by lying spirit demons. Stop looking up to them and you will recover your sight.

February 21

Mesmerized congregations observe pastor's sermon's like watching a theatrical stage play performance. The pastor performs his sermons with great emotional impact. It is not recorded in the Bible that crowds came to be "entertained" by apostles or saints fine sermons. Pastors today do whatever they want to do especially if it is unbiblical, they will do it.

February 22

Will you give up your golf sport for six months to share the gospel to the lost? Of course you won't. The Lord's yoke is easy. He doesn't ask you to do drastic things, but now He must insist you do as your last and final chance. Why? Your time has run out! You see, He wanted you to leave His Word at the golf courses, but you refused all these years. Thousands of golfers you could have reached will now go to hell because of you. And you are mistaken to believe that heaven awaits the disobedient? You and your false pastor will suffer the fate of those you lost. Justice will be served. Repent! Go share the gospel! Use gospel tracts if you do not know how to share the Good News of Salvation to the lost.

February 23

Gospel for sale! Pastors are in the gimcrack business of selling God's word to make profits. It is totally 100% unbiblical for pastors to sell the gospel regardless of the justification they give to excuse themselves. Nobody in the Bible dared to do it. Pastors shouldn't either, but they do!

February 24

Have you heard the strong, sop, soul soothing, brazen and courageous sermon lately? Now ask yourself how come these sermons are performed behind closed doors or in controlled environments? Did not Jesus speak in public? Everything is performed in a manner of strict control. Why aren't these wonderfully brave and competent speakers speaking in public? There is no money in it and they do not truly care to reach the lost, even if they say they do.

February 25

How much do you owe God for all the good things he has blessed you? When a pastor says this, the entire congregation often applauds loudly, but the pastor never talks to them on how to repay God with souls. Return the favor. Do something to save the lost, get personally involved in sharing the gospel. Reach out to the lost! That is what Christians do!

February 26

Churchgoing Christians that do not obey the Word of God have become or soon will be religious pagans serving a form of religion that is not endorsed by the Bible. This is what happens when you follow a pastor and not Jesus of Nazareth. You will love the pastor and despise obeying the Master.

February 27

Retired Christians. Look at the old man sitting in the fast food restaurant with not a care in the world. And that is his problem. He doesn't care to serve the Lord he professes to serve. This typical retired Christian is in prime country to leave gospel tracts by the thousands each month! But he is too busy doing nothing for the Lord. His pastor does not scold him or discipline his laziness as long as he keeps donating money to the collection basket. There is no accountability in the apostate church. Dead works are encouraged. It is a shameful abomination that retired Christians refuse to Work for the Lord to save the lost. Woe to those apostates who willfully forsake the Great Commission the Lord commanded us to do! Consider your ways. Repent and go bear much good fruit for God.

February 28

Soul winning is the most important duty and responsibility of a Christian. So why does your pastor not teach, instruct, or give sermons on how to reach the lost for Christ? Because he cares not for those heading to hell and that is the truth. Pastors have stolen the gospel and they intentionally keep it inside the closed doors of their church.

Two Months Passed and 10 More to Go!

Did you read, *The Lost Gospel of James*?

MARRIAGE CEREMONY

Of course it appears so right, but pastors have taken over this civic duty as if it were a Christian duty when it is not. In fact, it is not even Biblical or Christian and not mentioned in the Bible that "pastors" are to be conducting marriage ceremonies. It's true!

You think there is nothing wrong with this, but the danger is the pastor is weaseling into territory that is not of his Biblically instructed calling. He is out of bounds and has found a way to profit from selling his "religious services" to the gullible.

Business Opportunities

CHAPTER 3

Many Christians will be severely robbed not just in tithes, but when their pastor suddenly, and without warning, sells his church, retires and skips town. The church doors will be locked and all the money gone. It happens more than you are prepared to realize!

THE TICKET TRACT

On the following two pages is an example of my traffic ticket gospel tract. It is printed on yellow paper card stock and when placed on parked vehicles, well, it looks just like a parking ticket. And boy does it get read!

It's a sure fire way to grab the attention of these busy people going about their life not thinking of where they are heading eternally. It's a wake up call for them to get right before God, get saved and get to heaven and avoid hell. Because they will be judged and that's what this ticket tract emphasizes... judgement day!

Put these bright yellow tickets on parked cars and watch the results! You may think this may be cruel because the people do react at first thinking they just got a real ticket. Amazingly, despite the "comical" clip art on the ticket that a "real ticket would never have" the people still believe it is a real ticket. They sit in their car reading it, then they get to the back side and realize it's a gospel tract.

But that's what it takes today to get peoples' attention to make them see the light that there is a day of judgment coming and if they are not right with God, then His wrath is certainly upon them and it is hell to pay! In my view, *"It is cruel to remain silent and do nothing to share the gospel which most Christians choose as their daily mode of operation."* Are you one of these silent Christians too?

Jesus said to go proclaim the gospel to save the lost and this ticket tract is just one method a Christian may use. Be creative. You can write your own gospel tracts!

VIOLATION

Pursuant to Penal Code § 7. (i) (c) and (u) Violation of Motor Vehicles: operating a motor vehicle in a restrictive area duly posted as a no parking zone with or without an attempt to flee when pursued by duly appointed enforcement authorities.

AND

Pursuant to local ordnance §666.06 and §777.07 of the Superior Court requires a just fine with lawful punishment with a maximum term to serve shall be determined by the code enforcement magesterium.

AUTHORITY

Your vehicle and license plate was photographed by the automated security system authorized by the Department of Enforcement contracted by King Meter Maid Services is duly served upon you this day a violation ticket.

FLEEING JUSTICE

Because you fled from the scene, this warrant is duly served to bring you to justice.

PROMISE TO APPEAR

You promise to appear before the judge on the first Friday of the month at the court of jurisdiction herein addressed on the reverse side of this citation at 10:00 a.m. on the 3rd Floor, Suite 107, in Courtroom 'A'.

ATTORNEY BARRED

You may <u>NOT</u> attend with your lawyer. You may <u>NOT</u> protest your hearing. The automated system has proven your guilt beyond a reasonable doubt and there is no appeal. The righteous judge' decision is final.

YOUR RIGHTS

You have a limited right to contest this citation within seventy-two hours with proof your vehicle was a photo error created by the automated camera system. Be forewarned few errors occur. The photograph has your license plate including the driver clearly in the image.

Over...

TICKET

Violation   *Violation*

ERRORS
In the event the security system created an error beyond the control of the manufacturer resulting in a case of mistaken identity, you will be excused. However, such cases are rare. Be prepared to meet the judge.

PROCEDURES
Your day of appearance before the judge will be dramatic and you will have wished that you have not fled from the warnings given to you. The judge will ask you a series of questions about critical decisions you have made in your life then he will begin his proceeding to judge you for your actions. Absolutely no one will be permitted to speak on your behalf. No family members may testify. It will be you, standing alone before the judge of which he will not accept any explanations, excuses or hardship reasons to not punish you. The purpose of the court appearance is punitive and you will be punished according to the 'higher' law. You must submit a driver license and proof of citizenship. A birth record or social security card is acceptable. Failure to do so may enhance your punishment, as it upsets the judge and he will increase your grief. Be prepared!

SUBSTITUTION
Your day of appearance in court will require a search in the court's *Book of Life*. If your name appears in this book you will be freed from harm, the ticket will be destroyed, your record cleared and you may go your way saved from damnation of the law. The judge will forgive you and welcome you back into society. However, if your name is not found in the *Book of Life* you will wish you had accepted your substitute for the forgiveness of your sins. The judge will be forced to declare you guilty and serve severe punishment upon you.

WAIVED RIGHTS
You had your chance to accept the substitute who was ready and willing to take your place, so you would not suffer damnation. His name is Jesus Christ of Nazareth and you rejected his free gift. He planned to erase your sins, errors, mistakes and he desired to take the punishment for you. When you rejected him, your name was not found in the *Book of Life* and was placed into the *Book of Eternal Damnation*. This Judge makes and enforces the rules and those were His rules that you rejected and the price you will pay is brutal; a life of eternity in hell fire. You don't have to believe it to still end up in hell. The Bible says it is a fact that you will go to hell if you reject God's free gift of eternal life, Jesus of Nazareth. So it shall be.

LAST NOTICE
You are being given a second chance, by a concerned person, who truly cares about your eternal salvation by giving you this ticket to get your attention. Ask God to forgive you of your sins. Tell him you are sorry for breaking his laws and you want another chance to accept the sacrifice of His son, Jesus Christ of Nazareth, who died, shed his blood on a cross, rose from the dead for the remission of your sins. All it requires is a simple decision. Be forewarned, to not decide is a decision against Jesus and you will face that unforgiving judge.

NO THIRD CHANCE
You may laugh and joke now, but if you are wrong (and you know you have been wrong in this life) you may find yourself in hell for billions of years with no escape. That is what being saved is, to be saved from the torments of hell. Make the right choice! Get your name written in the Lamb's *Book of Life*... before it is too late!

Learn More **Tomorrow May Never Be**
Visit ➡ © JamesRussellPublishing.com

March 1

Are you a bastard? Your pastor won't likely preach or tell you this, but God only has sons or bastards and most church members today are not sons. You can read it in the Bible where God says this. What these playing-church-game pastors are performing creates disobedient children who are not even taught the true gospel. The flock does not even bother to read the Bible for themselves to seek truth and the ways of God. They don't even know what God hates and what He likes so they can never please Him; only invoke His anger and wrath. Find out what God likes and hates because your pastor is not going to tell you the whole truth; just a tad to deceive you and nothing more.

March 2

It is already the month of March. Time flies. In the last two months how many cults have you exposed to save those being misled by deceiving pastors? How many gospel tracts have you left here and there in the past sixty days? How many sermons has your pastor performed to instruct you to do these things? When will you begin to bear good fruit for the Lord? It must begin now or you never will.

March 3

The true gospel is not to be found inside your church today. It will not come forth behind closed doors. It will not be anywhere to be found in your church because the true gospel is what Jesus spoke. It is his words, not the fabulous stories, cunningly devised fables, fabrications and outright lies pastors pour out upon the congregations. Matt. 4:23, Mark 1:14. The doctrine of the saints is based upon the Words of Jesus and they believed him and obeyed his words. Are you obeying Jesus or your church? 99.999% of churchgoers obey their pastor and not Jesus.

March 4

Doctrine means "teaching" so read II John 1:9 *"Whosoever transgresses and abides not in the doctrine of Christ, hath not God."* Are you really obeying Jesus? Are you sharing the gospel to the lost? Then write it down to see your productivity or stop lying to yourself. Giving money to proclaim the gospel is no excuse and no substitute for obedience to the Lord's commands. Too many Christians are openly disobeying the Lord and being blessed by their apostate pastors.

March 5

Do not think that you will escape hell's eternal fire if you are deceived by a wolf in sheep's clothing. Jesus gave you a clear warning and a command, *"Do not be deceived..."* Go read it in the Bible before your pastor side-tracts you with another brilliant sermon.

March 6

Don't let pastors fool you with their camouflaged "outreach ministry." It is a recruiting tool to increase church membership, not to save the lost. The sole purpose is to recruit under the guise of performing the Great Commission. Beware! You will not satisfy the Lord's commands working to increase church membership for your pastor.

March 7

Pastor that owns his church has a serious conflict of interest.

March 8

Jesus warned you that hirelings are dangerous. They do not care for the flock. Is your pastor a hireling? Who is paying him? Beware! When Jesus says a thing, you had better have ears to hear what He is saying. Your paid pastor is who Jesus was identifying. You need to keep a very sharp eye on the hireling. Jesus warned about those making a living on the expense of the sheep. If you are fooled it is your fault. Be wise as a serpent!

March 9

Jesus saves without your church and without church membership required and falling away has nothing to do with a person no longer attending your church. In fact, that person may go forth witnessing to the lost leaving you all to continue playing church. You have a lot to unlearn. Jesus knew of two working for him and they were not part of the assembly and Jesus said they were for him, not against him. In fact, a person who evangelizes on a daily basis would backslide joining your church. Is your church members witnessing to the lost on a routine basis? Show the proof? You will be judged by your works not by your faith. Matt. 16:27, Rom. 2:6; Rev. 20:12, 13. Your pastor forgot to preach on this too?

March 10

Jokes in the pulpit and fantastic stories meant to entertain the congregation are designed to disarm the gullible; to let your guard down. You will see none of these control tactics used in the Bible, so pastors have no right to use any controlling device to influence the flock's emotions or thoughts, but this activity is now commonplace inside churches of all denominations.

March 11

The first sermon message John the Baptist spoke was "repent" and Jesus first sermon was also expressed, "repent". The first message from pastors today is anything but repent. Many preach how to get rich or teach of end time events or how Christians should be more blessed and happier, or whatever, but repentance of sin is avoided as if it were sin itself.

March 12

Pastors preach of a new kingdom of God when they distort the Bible and make certain the flock remains faithful and obedient to him and his church. Read I Sam. 8:4-22. The Israelites also rejected the Lord by demanding a kingdom that was inferior and the Lord gave them their king in His anger. Is your pastor your king? Don't be too quick to deny it. Most Christians listen, follow and obey their pastor way more than they obey Jesus. It is sad and true. John 14:23.

March 13

The pastor pumps you up in his sermon to get ready to be blessed and to expect it! You will notice one thing is missing. He never teaches you how you can share your blessings with the lost. God sees this as absolute nonsense. The Bible teaches that those who bless others with mercy shall be blessed in mercy in return. You don't need a pastor's sermon to inflate your emotions to focus on greed and selfishness. You go be a blessing to others first and let the Lord Himself reward you.

March 14

Will you dare to skip going to church this week to share the gospel with the lost? Will you? The Lord wants the lost to be saved and sadly church attendance always takes priority over what God wants. You won't even give up one day? Keep this rejection up and you will be cut off the vine. Church attendance does not save and does not save the lost and it does not bear much good fruit; not according to the Bible.

March 15

Who is the last person you can name who you shared the knowledge of God's Kingdom to? If nobody comes to mind you are not alone. Most Christians never witness to the lost. Who teaches them to disobey the Lord? Their pastor does. You can disobey your pastor by becoming a soul winner for Christ, but you are not much interested. You must follow the Good Shepherd or you will never bear much good fruit. Ezek. 33:6.

March 16

What was the gospel Jesus commanded the apostles and the seventy disciples? To go to church, obey your pastor, be loyal to your church and support it financially, endure to the end and you will be saved! This is the bill of goods pastors have used to mislead, control and fleece the sheep. The true gospel is to go forth and proclaim the Kingdom of God. This is what your pastor does not want you to do. A ministry of your own is what God wills for all believers! Pastors do not share God's vision therefore they refuse to teach you how. The lost just keep on being lost. Read Acts19:8, 20:25, 28:23, 28:30. Gal1:8. Matt24:14.

March 17

Has anyone in your church personally distributed twenty-five thousand gospel tracts in the past 5 years? Does that sound like a lot of tracts? It's only fourteen tracts a day! How many could you do? How about one tract per day? You can't do that either? Why not? Isn't it time you obey the Lord to share the gospel to the lost? How can your pastor think it is okay to disobey the Lord and not demand obedience to His commands?

Your pastor could even finance this ministry, but he is not interested in the things of God. Are you? Will you?

March 18

Imagine the apostles not only had to walk out on their Jewish religion they had to also stop assembling with the Jews and abandon their church and temple worship. So it is today you also must walk away from the apostate church and the wolf pastor leading a false assembly titled a "worship service". Does this shock you? It shouldn't, it is clearly stated in the Bible, *"Be ye not unequally yoked together with unbelievers"* 2 Cor.6:14. Most Christians ignore and disobey this command. Are you so addicted to church obedience/attendance that you no longer hear the Lord?

March 19

Pastors are growing their churches with pagans, sinners and unsaved people polluting the church in the process. Why? It is to make more money for themselves. Predators invade the assembly of sheep.

March 20

Pastors are good at being clever. They donate money (your money you gave him) for social causes and even missions. Maybe even a whopping million dollars or two or more. Beware! The pastor is not in the church business to give money away. The congregation is being duped, as the pastor pocketed the ninety-percent or more that was given to him. Christian evangelist preachers do the same. It is somewhat legal if you gave him the money, but illegal if the pastor lied by concealing how much he was keeping for himself. Demand an accounting! If you were deceived, demand a full refund! But the tax and giving to charity laws make it very hard to sue to get your money back from churches. The law favors the pastor! And pastors are very careful to follow the law, but they can still rob you by taking your tithe money which is not a New Testament Christian obligation.

DARE TO CHALLENGE YOUR LEADERS

If you don't dare to challenge your church leaders and hold their feet to the fire, they will run you down into the earth without mercy. You will become a dedicated, faithful fun-loving churchgoer and that is all you will ever be.

They will lie to you and your eyes will become foggy and you will only believe what they tell you to believe. You will go with the flow and think all is well. That's how the cults operate and the churches are doing the same thing as other churches are doing to capture their audience.

But be prepared. If you make too many waves you will be excommunicated from the pastor's church and that will set you free to go work for the Lord to do what is important to Him... saving the lost.

What good is your church membership if souls are being lost to hell while you do nothing to save them? What good is it?

Hmmm, I shall preach this sermon to them this Sunday and not one will have the desire to go save the lost for Christ, not one. Yes, this is <u>my will</u>.

LEAVE THE CHURCH

Oh, such a horrible thought! How could you say such a thing? Well, did it ever occur to you that the apostles had to leave their church to follow Jesus? Didn't Jesus say to them to come and follow him? Oh, yes he did. They had to give up their church and their pastors (church leaders) and dare to follow the Lord. And Jesus said if they looked back, they were not worthy of him.

Today, you need to also leave your church to escape from the influence of the apostate church system so you can follow Jesus and the Holy Spirit so you can do the will of the Father. Because <u>only those who do the will of the Father go to heaven</u>. Matt 7:21. Read your Bible!

In truth, the will of the Father is for you to get out from these manipulating, controlling, do nothing for God do all for the pastor churches and *go* save the lost. That is your Christian duty, not just be a churchgoer. The choice is yours. Who will you follow and obey? If you are like the majority you will choose your pastor over Jesus and remain in your church and you will bear no good fruit.

March 21

The Bible demands that you not associate with disobedient brethren. Read 2 Thes. 3:14. That means you are to leave any church or assembly of disobedient brethren, permanently. If church members are not personally and actively proclaiming the gospel to the lost and they insist on and/or make excuses for disobeying the Lord's commands, you must leave them. Are you leaving?

March 22

Disobeying the Lord's commands is equal to denying Jesus before men and renouncing your faith for all to see. Why bother to be a Christian when you do not serve and obey the Lord? You only worship in vain. It is more honorable to obey the Lord over and above your church and pastor. Jesus is first or none at all. That's the way it is. Who are you disobeying? Pick one, pick two, but serve and obey the Lord above all and without compromise!

March 23

Read II Chron. 36:15,16. Anyone who dares to challenge the apostate pastor will be mocked and despised and the congregation will rally behind the false pastor in full support. The end result is rejection of the warning of God and there will be no remedy. Be careful to follow the Lord. You must reject the wolf or you will be standing against God Himself.

March 24

Beware of pastors that are uniting believers with unbelievers. A believer believes and obeys the Word of God (KJV Bible) not their pastor's teachings no matter how sweet to the ears his words may sound. You can not be unequally yoked with false teachers. Read 2 Jn. 7-11. Get out of the church while there is still time to escape.

March 25

Your pastor has no special powers or a special direct communication link to God. Don't you fall for that old trick! Pastors use it to elevate themselves above the congregation so they can control them. Gifts can be given by God but He never singles out just the pastor and excludes the saints. If a pastor has a special power, be very careful. Even great oratory leadership skill can be a false power.

March 26

What does you pastor really want? What is his true motivation and purpose? Is he teaching everyone to obey Jesus' commands? Does he give instructions on how to save the lost? Does he get his hands dirty going downtown to proclaim the gospel? What is he really doing? Playing church? He's too busy to save the lost? His church needs come before the Lord's commands? Most all pastors today fall into these traps. Reading about apostasy will give you the knowledge and wisdom to see and expose it.

March 27

If you stop attending church worship services, you will fall away and be devoured by Satan, because you have no pastor to protect you. This is a lie pastors have pushed hard to keep you in their apostate church. God commands you to leave apostasy! You are commanded to come out. It is better to walk out of the congregation of disobedient brethren than to stay and disobey the Lord.

March 28

Why should the Lord grant the desire of the apostate's prayer? He doesn't. He will not hear your prayer due to your sin. That alone is a good reason to get out of any apostasy.

March 29

Whose will be done? Is it the will of the Father or the will of your church? Only those who do the will of the Father shall be saved, so when it comes down to it, make sure you are obeying God's Word and disobey your pastor if you must. Never compromise. Read the Bible and obey what you read, but don't ever ignore the Lord's will no matter what your pastor tells you (or doesn't tell you).

March 30

A pastor is not going to tell you to disobey the Lord. He will get you to disobey by his golden silence. If he does not teach you how to obey the Lord's commands he is apostate. If he does not preach the blood of Christ he is apostate, but if he preaches the latter and ignores the prior he is a false teacher. What is your pastor not telling you? Find out by reading what Jesus is telling you to do. You will find many things your pastor is hiding from your eyes.

March 31

When you are in need, do you run to your pastor? Prosperity, supply whatever you desire, run to your pastor. When danger threatens, run to your pastor. This is what pastors want you to do. They substitute as God and this is an abomination that has infected all churches controlled by a pastor. The Lord is not your pastor, so why do you idolize him as your earthly Lord and savior? Read Isaiah 45:22, *"Look unto me, and be ye saved, all the ends of the earth."* Why then do you still go to your pastor when in need?

Another Month Passed and 9 More to Go!

Just don't disagree with your pastor!
He will convince you the Bible is wrong and he
is right.

CHAPTER 4

You say I am too hard on the pastors? Jesus was too hard dealing with Pharisees and Teachers of the Law? Spare no mercy in exposing the false, lying pastor. Stand up and expose them so others may be saved. It is too unkind to remain silent, is it not? Hell does not wait.

MONEY TRACT

Below are samples of my money tract. When folded in half lengthwise, the front side of the tract appears as a full size $100 bill. People quickly, without delay, pick it up where ever they find it. When they unfold the bill they read the back message. It is a powerful tool to "wake people up" to the facts. I used to use soft, loving messages in my gospel tracts, but not anymore. It is time to get tough and tell it like it is. If you are not saved you are going to hell. <u>That is the message Jesus and the apostles preached</u>, but today nobody wants to preach the truth because it may offend people.

Front Side

Back Side

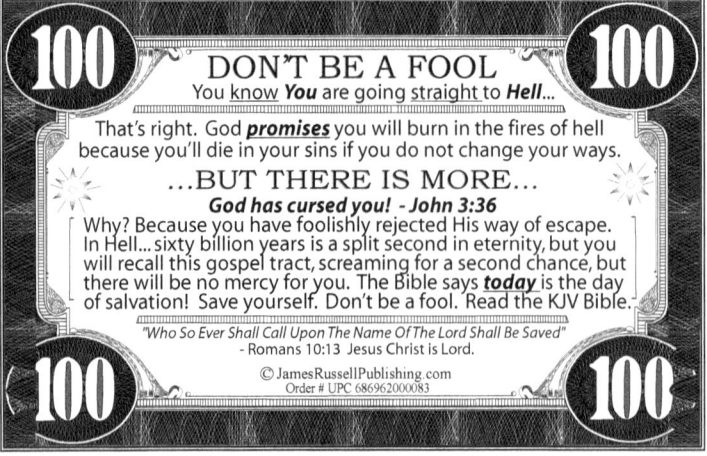

April 1

You have read James 1:7 about being double-minded and you will receive nothing from the Lord. When you divide your devotion between the Lord and your church you are now, by default, devoting yourself to your pastor. You are trying to serve two masters. No wonder the Christian churchgoers have become beggars before the Lord. Nobody loudly promises they will go forth to proclaim the gospel to the lost. It's a selfish worship service so popular today.

April 2

Reverend. This improper title really means respectful which even God does not deem to be respectful to no man. It also means admiring. Do you see the danger? Pastors are not above the flock and they are not to be respected as being special, adored or worshipped. Call the pastor by the Biblical name, "Pastor" no more, no less. He is not your father.

April 3

Beware of those who wear religious costumes. Yes, the fine robes that gives you the impression that person is special and privileged to be dressed unlike the congregation. This is a deliberate act of psychological manipulation. Not even Jesus wore special robes to inject authority on others. Shame on pastors who wear special clothing inside their church! It is not Christian.

April 4

What would Jesus do? He would pick up a whip and scourge your pastor, overturn the money collection baskets and scream scoldings of the apostasy taking place. Jesus would never react with loving favor to a disobedient church meeting together in his name. Don't be so eager for his coming! Repent and obey the Lord. Are you spreading the gospel?

April 5

Your pastor may teach you to be lovely toward sinners, but the Bible gives you stern warning to not do so. *"...If there come any unto you, and bring not this doctrine, receive him not into your house, neither bid him*

WRITING BOOKS

Have you noticed how pastors take your money then invest it in writing and selling books, DVD's and other products? How convenient for them to use the faithful's money as a free loan of which he has no intention of paying back! He keeps all the profits for himself and makes you think you are doing God's work. This is not Biblical and it is not Christian. Collections of money were taken in the New Testament to be "shared" among the brethren in need! Never did a pastor pull such scams to fool the people and rob them of their money. Read your Bible... it's true!

CAN A PASTOR SEND A MAN TO HELL?

Jesus warned that those who follow the blind leader will all fall into the pit. Yes, they will follow their pastor right into the bowels of hell because they dared not defy their pastor or dare to disbelieve him. They trusted, heard and obeyed their pastor, not Jesus. They tried to serve both Jesus and their pastor master. It won't work!

God speed: For he that biddeth him God speed is partaker of his evil deeds" 2 John 1:9-11. That's what your Bible says, so be careful that you obey the Word or you will be partaking in evil.

April 6

Should you curse those who reject Jesus? What would your pastor say? Ask him. Saint Paul said, *"Let him be accursed."* What are you really learning in your church? If you distribute a gospel tract he may tell you you have now fallen from grace for now you are relying on "works" and not "grace". He preaches a cheap grace bearing no good works. Are you being duped?

April 7

Is your pastor giving the church money for humanitarian assistance? Is he giving money to poor pagans? If so, he is grossly mismanaging the money. Paul took collections of money to share with "poor believers" not poor pagans. Why is your pastor ignoring the many poor believers, yet he feels it is okay to give church money to pagans? The Bible is the blueprint of Christian instruction and example. Too many pastors are misleading the flock damaging believers and blessing unrepentant sinners. Believers come first, not last and never should be excluded. Never! Pastor, give back the money to the believers!

April 8

Incompetent pastors are creating horrific damage to the church. They do what they want to do, not what God expects and commands them to do. When the flock remains silent, the pastor leads and the sheep follow him to destruction. Pastors should not have absolute power and control. That is why many "own" their own church buildings, to remain in absolute power. Many even have loyal elders in their pocket that will never dare defy him. The pay and honor is much too tempting. All are hirelings! Beware. They are everywhere!

April 9

You have seen it hundreds of times as the pastor takes on the role of Jesus giving a "sermon" to razzle and dazzle the flock. Most Christians attend church just to experience the sermon. It is a prime-time event and it is even televised, duplicated and sold to make profits. Only Jesus attracted crowds and only Jesus gave formal sermons and he never sold them. None of the apostles or disciples gave sermons. Think about that! Apostasy is a mixture of a false gospel and disobedience wrapped into a sweet-smelling counterfeit of the real thing. When the main event is to stop everything and all ears and eyes are focused on the pastor, he is stealing Jesus' glory and honor. Paul wrote with power but was meek, shy in public.

April 10

When you read the KJV Bible, ask if what you see the early church doing is what your church is doing. Now you will see how prolific apostasy has infiltrated deeply into the church. It will frighten you! Rev. 12:17.

April 11

Are there any good pastors left? Yes, but not many to be found and most will be so busy preaching the gospel to the lost they have no time for the church-crowd. Some are missionaries; some are hospital chaplains, prison ministers. But the average pastor today is apostate by choice, by ignorance, by incompetence or by denominational orders. The typical church is the deadliest places you can be today. The great falling away is upon you!

April 12

The Old Testament prophets angrily blasted apostates. In the New Testament Jesus (Matt. 23:14-33) and later his apostles verbally condemned the churchmen apostates damning them to hell even calling them accursed. Today the Lord has a few obedient servants exposing apostates, but way too few. Now it is time for the rubber to meet the road. Why is your pastor silent on the apostasy issue? Because he wants you to believe apostasy does not exist or that it does not roost nearby or within his church. Where is the pastoral training on how to detect false teachers? Why is your pastor ignoring the apostasy issues? Is he teaching you how to contend for the faith once given to the saints? Start asking why. Apathy is the disease nobody cares about.

April 13

If someone, even your pastor, teaches a different gospel, it is no gospel at all. Paul said it. This means all of your church attendance is in vain and of zero value in God's eyes. You have wasted a lifetime of church membership remaining in an apostate church or system. What does your pastor do in his spare time? Most church members don't know. Does he share the gospel with the lost in town? Don't count on it! Time to come out!

April 14

Is your pastor preaching a different Jesus? Of course not! They would never do such a thing and the church would see it right away. Hold on to your seat. The Bible said false teachers will come into the church to devour the flock. Paul said they would even preach *another* Jesus.

April 15

Preaching another Jesus is a perfect trick. This Jesus loves all things with politeness and kindness toward habitual hard-core sinners, never scolding so as never to offend. He tolerates sin, accepts idol worship and loves churchgoers in any spiritual condition, blesses those who disobey him and this wonderful Jesus gives his pastors all authority to his church. The real Jesus is no longer preached in churches today. Even Jesus commands are ignored, set aside, discarded and trampled under foot. Pastors are to be closely watched.

April 16

You cannot discipline or fire a pastor who owns the deed to his church. He now has immunity from Biblical discipline and that is not Biblical at all. Many pastors have sold their church and ran off to greener pastures all without warning. The congregation arrives only to find the doors locked. It happens more than you think. Jesus said to be wise, so find out who owns your church. Remember, church ownership is not Biblical.

April 17

Where do apostate pastors come from? From apostate churches, and they then attend apostate seminary schools and then they start new apostate churches. The system has grown so huge that apostate churches now are the mainstream and appear as normal.

April 18

A man feels God calling him to build a church… a physical church of course, which he will own as a real estate investment. Wrong! Not once has God told anyone to build a place of worship in the New Testament. Even the great Temple was utterly destroyed! Jesus never authorized anyone to build a church building. The apostles and Ddsciples never did. If it were okay they would have said to do it. They never did build a church. The moment a church building is built it is the seed of wrongdoing, a foundation on sand.

April 19

Jesus commanded us to go forth in public places to proclaim the gospel. Today pastors (super men of the cloth) only proclaim a gospel inside their church behind closed doors. Something is very wrong with this picture. He will teach you church attendance is bearing good fruit, but the Bible never says this.

April 20

Talking about apostasy will always appear to have a unchristian sting and there simply is no polite way to expose it. Jesus harshly scolded the apostate scribes and Pharisees often Matt. 3:7 23:27, 23:33, 12:34. Read Acts 7:51-53 and Jeremiah 48:10 are just a "few" examples. In fact it is these very verses apostates choose to ignore and pastors' stubbornly refuse to preach, so they preach a "different" gospel that is no gospel at all. That is dangerous.

April 21

Is your pastor a devil worshipper? Of course not, you say. Is he a member of a secret society? Has he denied Christ? Is he commingling with pagans? Find out and quick! To join the Masons you must deny Christ as you proclaim in the ritual that you are in darkness and you come to masonry to obtain light! Jesus said he was the light of the world - John

8:12. This is just one example. Secret societies are dangerous to the Christian especially when a pastor is a loyal member. Learn more at www.chick.com. Search out books that expose secret social groups.

April 22

Millions of Christians have joined pagan secret societies. Secret rituals, secret meetings, secret oaths, secret symbols, secret signals, and secret secrets will never be Christian and only serve to compromise the Christian participating in secrets. Jesus said nothing should be done in secret as He will expose them. Many apostate pastors are inviting and encouraging others to join these secret groups that despise Jesus.

April 23

Pastors have created a secret society in which there is a code of loyalty that they will not expose the sins of another pastor, and they will in no way interfere with a false teacher/pastor deceiving a congregation. Pastors are not warning their believers of false gospels, false religions, damning heresies, etc. They remain as silent cowards, shameful false Christians terrified if they tell the truth another pastor may expose them!

April 24

What does the word Laodicea mean to you? Most pastors are guilty of it, so better to find out now before it is too late for you to escape!

April 25

It is not popular to expose apostasy. It takes courage and a determined will to obey the Lord above the expectations of man and even family and friends. Many Christians wish they can be used by God, but they cower with fright knowing to do so may cause others to not like them. In that case they rather not serve God. They rather be popular and serve their church or pastor or both. And, to obey God, they may even have to expose their own pastor and that can lead to the horrible rejection and excommunication from the apostate church. They do not want the Lord's freedom but prefer darkness and bondage. Is that you?

April 26

Homosexual pastors? Since when did the Bible declare such acts are not sin? Imagine that tens of thousands of Christians have not left such churches; they are still loyal to it and financially support it. Compromise is abandonment from the Lord! The apostate church is stronger than you think it is. It has power to keep you inside apostate churches and under the subjection of abominable pastors permitting sin to invade the church.

April 27

Christian bookstore idols? Ministry gift items are idols? Don't buy them and install them inside your home. Behind every idol is a demon! Get rid of the idols inside your home. Destroy each and every single image. Smash them to pieces! Statues, pictures of Jesus, crucifixes, etc. The Bible makes it clear, they are idols. (It pained me to destroy my idols and images of heavenly things, angels, photos, etc., but ultimately I am glad I did). Obey the Lord. Why do things that you know upset Him? Why put things inside your home you know He hates? Jesus of the Bible will never walk inside a building with idols. Don't kid yourself, he won't do it.

April 28

Cheer up! Yes, some Christian bookstores do sell false Gospels, perverted Bibles, witchcraft, heavenly images and outright idols forbidden by the Second Commandment, but it's still yet to come... Christian brothels! On second thought the apostate church may already be doing this when pastors fail to reprimand and discipline known adulterers including fornicators living together unmarried? Is the church also the new dating game? A meeting place for homosexuals, lesbians, whore-mongerers? Are you a member of such a sin-tolerant church? If so, why are you? Who is pastoring such a church?   The true Biblical Jesus of the Bible sure isn't.

April 29

Is your pastor urging you to submit written complaints about filthy subject matter on over-the-air, cable, satellite television shows and commercials? How about video games? Your pastor has great influence over the congregation and he should be proactive to speak out in a positive way. Why is it he does not care? Sermons demanding action is useless.

The church needs hands-on pastors. Or is he afraid he could lose his tax-exempt status? The foundation of the modern church is horrifically flawed when pastors must remain silent to protect their skin if they speak out on sin. He should not "own" a church building and he would not be in such slavery to the state.

April 30

Filth in the home is a subject pastors avoid and the average church member would embarrass Christ if Jesus were to visit their home and find filthy movies, pagan books and magazines also with foul language and photos, etc. Their walls and shelves loaded with idols and images. It is no wonder they have so many troubles. They have compromised and invited Satan and his demons into their home. Pastors should inspect church member's homes to see the rot and filth and teach compliance to Biblical standards. The congregation should permit such inspections for their own good. At least sermons should be focused on such matters and not ignored.

A Month Has Passed. 8 More to Go!

THE CROOKED FOUNDATION

The cute little church building we see is actually the great falling away masterpiece by design. From this building it empowers a pastor to take over, actually hijack Christians and lure them into obeying him and his denomination. Complete control over the flock takes place and "fellowshipping" is destroyed as all eyes look forward toward the pastor, not each other. Then to avoid paying taxes the pastor agrees to not preach the entire true Bible or warn the flock of dangers, etc. The apostles never built one physical church building and they changed the world!

A Crooked Foundation Can Never Be Made Straight. Church Buildings Are Not New Testament Christianity. Never Has Been, Never Will Be.

CHAPTER 5

SILENT CHRISTIANS

The Bible condemns those who are silent and refuse to stand up for God and turn their eyes away. There is no such thing as a silent Christian in the Bible, but today we have millions of silent Christians not taking on the battle to push back the darkness. They choose to go to church each week as their duty. But to save the lost, they say, is not their calling. They employ every excuse imaginable to circumvent Jesus' commission to go save the lost. They refuse to do it!

ATTENTION

CHRISTIAN BUSINESSMEN

On the next two pages you can see an example on how you, as a true Christian, can reach the lost and advertise your business at the same time.

Too many Christian business owners are advertising their business and not advertising the gospel of Jesus Christ. They live secret lives as Christians, but <u>advertise like hell for their business</u>.

On the front side of my advertising is a gospel tract and on the back side is an ad to advertise my Web site. In this way I am reaching out to the lost while advertising my business at the same time. And on my business Web site I have a Christian site too!

There's two ways to look at this. Some will say you are using the gospel to sell your product. Others with will say it is sharing the gospel and better than businesses that don't. Your motive is the most important to consider and that will be judged between you and the Lord on the day of judgement.

I believe a Christian who owns a business is obligated to share his business with His Lord and to use his business to reach the lost for Christ. How many Christian businesses have waiting rooms and counter tops that are void of gospel tracts? Too many! These devoted churchgoing Christian businessmen have <u>evicted the Lord from their business life</u>! And they do it for fear of "losing customers" offending their customers with the gospel. And that is the truth of the matter! They are ashamed of the gospel!

If you run a business then use it for the Lord's glory. Let Him in and use your business to reach the lost. And if you offend customers so what? The Lord can create new customers to those who are faithful to him.

DID YOU KNOW?

Believe it or Not!

YOU MAY BE A RELIGIOUS PAGAN !!!

Don't Laugh! The Bible May Prove You Wrong... Dead Wrong!

CHRISTIANITY today has fallen so far away from the Bible Jesus would not even be able to recognize it. Let's look at a few of these changes...

TITHE Jesus and his Apostles never authorized a pastor to collect any tithe money because the tithe is Old Testament Biblical but it is not Christian. Not one tithe was collected. Pastors have no Biblical authority to collect any tithe money, period!

NEVER did Jesus or his Apostles, and even Saint Paul who was the greatest church builder, never told anyone to build a church building. They never even desired it, wanted it or needed it. They met in homes.

PASTOR is not to lord it over the flock or to be the main attraction or to conduct sermons, weddings, funerals, etc. Read your Bible, none of these things are permissible or authorized. No Biblical authority is granted. Read the Bible and you will see the truth.

BIBLE STUDY will never reveal these truths to you or your children. They are intentionally skipped over to pull the wool over your eyes, so you may continue to be fleeced by the apostate church system.

  Over...

CHECK OUT THIS WEB SITE...

POWERFUL BOOKS TO HELP YOU
We have the books to help you succeed!

and

MANY HELPFUL FREE ARTICLES
Here's just a few...

ADVICE FOR BOOK AUTHORS
Everybody wants to write a book, yet few do! They don't think it will sell. Wrong! Go to a bookstore and look at all the books being sold. You can too! Free advice for book authors on our Web site. Get started today!

ADVICE FOR SCREENWRITERS
Imagine writing your own television or movie script and getting paid six figures for selling it? It happens all of the time. Tired of seeing lousy movies? Then write your own! Free advice on our Web site. Now it the time. Hollywood needs scripts!

ADVICE FOR TARGET SHOOTERS
Check out our free professional level target shooting lessons for shotgun shooters. Shoot rifle and pistol? Check out our new book that will let you take tax deductions on all your sporting equipment. Even ammo, gasoline, auto repairs, furniture and much more! You save thousands of dollars each and every year! Find out how on our Web site!

ADVICE FOR CHRISTIANS
Learn why the end is nearer than you think it is! Discover who the false and lying pastors are that was predicted in the Bible to come in the last days. Many articles to enlighten and frighten, but you must know the truth before it is too late.

RIDE A MOTORCYCLE?
Read our free motorcycle articles and check out our motorcycle books and movies on our Web site. Ride a Harley? You can save a ton of money with Harley-Davidson book in oil changes and repairs, etc. Learn how to buy a motorcycle with our free articles on our Web site that will save you thousands of dollars!

VISIT US... SEE WHAT WE HAVE FOR YOU!
© LEARN MORE! Go To: JamesRussellPublishing.com

Give the Gift of Life

The stakes are high. Very high! Heaven or an eternity in hell awaits you, your family, relatives, friends, and church members! You can reach them! Give them these pages, so they too can make an informed decision to follow the Lord! It is the least you can do. You owe it to them!

May 1

Paul mentions (in Galatians 3:1); he asks, *"Who has bewitched you?"* ...a scolding to those who have turned from the true gospel. You also must turn from your rebellious ways and return to the true gospel because rebellion is the sin of witchcraft 1 Samuel 15:23. You listen too much to your pastor's teachings and not to Jesus, "He that heareth My word... has everlasting life..." John 5:24. Your pastor is not preaching the entire gospel. Read Jesus' words and diligently do what he tells you to do!

May 2

It's not always what your pastor preaches that is false; it's what he does not preach that will absolutely lead you astray! All he has to do to create another Jesus and another gospel is to simply not preach or teach the entire gospel of Christ. It's an old trick that fools millions straight into hell.

May 3

The more pastor sermons you listen to, the more you will be exchanging the truth of the gospel for a lie, if you are not careful to verify what you hear as being an accurate interpretation of the true gospel of Christ. You will be deceived otherwise. Pastors cannot be trusted. They have taught heresies and false Gospels to the destruction of millions upon millions of people. Read the KJV Bible.

May 4

Does your Bible have the words "Holy Bible" on the cover or in the title pages? If so you may be reading a perverted version used by apostate pastors, false teachers and cults to deceive. Is your pastor using such a Bible to teach you? The King James Version (KJV) is the one to read, believe and obey.

May 5

The Lord is totally fed up with apostates. He tells the believer to warn them, but God has already given up on them. You can read this in the Bible that God gives them up to believe strong delusions and lies. It's happening before your very eyes inside most churches where pastors spin fables of a different Jesus, a different Father, a different Spirit and proclaiming a different gospel

May 6

Jesus said it clearly, *"Call no man father."* If you do this you challenge Jesus and openly judge him to be a liar. Jesus said not to do it! Catholics do this like a bad habit. I know, I was one once!

May 7

Did you know the Roman Catholics changed the Ten Commandments? The Second Commandment, telling us not to create idols, has been removed so statues and images can be sold. Bottom line, it is better for you to destroy the idols in your home and stop honoring them or face the fury of the Lord.

May 8

Christian retreats are often located in prime vacation areas. There is one thing they refuse to do and that is to share the gospel to the lost in the community where these retreats exist. Secret things go on in these retreats, selfish things to please themselves while the lost perish nearby. The Baptists own a retreat in the Black Hills of South Dakota where a tourist steam train passes about four times each day. Not one sign or a billboard of a Bible verse exists to reach tens of thousands for Christ. A simple sign is needed, but the Christians are too busy resting and partying to save the lost. They have "retreated" from Jesus.

May 9

Is this a true simple statement of Christianity? *"Danger, it is hell without Jesus."* The Bible says it is so that all who reject Jesus will go to hell, so if you don't have Jesus you can expect hell. Right? Now make some signs with those words and put them on the front door of your church. Your pastor will become enraged and he will remove it. Why? Because he fears "the truth" will offend people! You will see this pattern of behavior repeat itself at any church of your choosing. Is your pastor removing such signs? He should be putting them up all over town!

May 10

Ask your pastor to finance your tract distribution ministry to reach the lost for Christ and he will refuse. If he accepts he will soon cancel the program. Excuses will be given, as pastors do not want members of the church to have their own ministries. It cuts into his profits and other church programs that saves few to nobody.

May 11

How is it that pastors and their followers can be so selfish not to share eternal life with others? You can't find any of these professed Christians on any given day actively sharing the gospel to the lost. You can't find any evidence of their presence in the community. Gospel tracts can't be found. Courthouse area you can't find them. They refuse to witness in public places. Powerful preaching takes place behind closed doors or sealed TV studios preaching to Christians. They want to keep eternal life to themselves! Go share it.

May 12

Real church growth is one pastor raiding the flock of another, one denomination blending into another. Pastors creating programs and events to attract, lure and ultimately create more pew warming Christians to join "his church" that is not the church Jesus founded or authorized. The apostate church never follows the Biblical example and the fruits are different and counterfeit.

May 13

Go to a major sports event, fair, vehicle rally or other community event and look for the pastors and churchgoers. They are there, in disguise going about not the Master's business. It is a golden opportunity to reach the lost with the gospel, but they don't give a hoot. Such is the fruit of the apostates.

May 14

Have you found a gospel tract at the zoo, or a theme park, or a bowling alley, at a supermarket, a casino, a department store or shopping mall? Why is it you are not leaving tracts everywhere you go?

May 15

Jesus preached and never sold his gospel. Pastors do! Paul was a prolific writer and never wrote and sold his book. Pastors do! The apostles and disciples planted and built churches, but they never built a physical church. Pastors do! They never "owned" a church. Pastors do! They never took church money for their own wealth. Pastors do! The list goes on and on. Apostasy grows like a weed taking over the entire garden choking out the truth until the lie appears acceptable.

May 16

Disobey your pastor! If your pastor is silent on the subject that all Christians should be distributing gospel tracts, then disobey him! Shame and dishonor on that pastor. Go, obey Jesus; *"The Good Shepherd"* who wants you to share eternal life with the lost! Your pastor teaches that doing the will of God, but what he teaches is not the will of God as spelled out in the Bible. Beware!

May 17

Pastors are responsible for the great falling away from the gospel of Jesus Christ. They are responsible for the prolific rise of crime, prostitution and every filthy vice. The Old and New Testament proves this to be true over and over again. The people fall away and perish when the apostates come into authority and God pours out his wrath. Stop following pastors! Follow Jesus! Stop obeying pastors! Obey Jesus!

May 18

Going to church is not salvation and never will be according to the

LEARN TO DOUBT

Better to doubt your pastor than risk him being wrong and taking you to hell. It is better to obey the Lord and disobey your pastor and start being a "doer of the Word of God" instead of a hearer that your pastor wants you to be. Somebody is wrong, and it ain't God!

Start questioning everything you see, hear and do inside that church building and start asking if this is what Jesus really told you to do in his Bible. Did he really tell us to go to church each and every week on Sunday? Did he tell pastor's to build expensive church buildings? Did he tell pastor's to take money from Jesus' followers for his own consumption? Did he tell us to obey our pastors? Did he say it is his will that we blindly obey our pastors' and to fall into a pit with him?

What did Jesus really say? What did he tell you do do? If he told you to go save the lost then why are you not doing so? Who has convinced you that it is okay to disobey Jesus? Could it be your pastor? Could it be him? By his very silence on this subject that is what he is preaching to you! He has taught you to be a disobedient brethren to the Lord, yet very obedient to his wishes, whims and demands.

Jesus said you should go fishing for men, but you don't. It is amazing how pastors seem to forget about the important things Jesus wants you do be doing for him. Your pastor says, "Go to church." Jesus say's to go fish for men's souls. We all know who you are serving! Wise up and get to work.

THE PASTOR'S LIES

The moment a pastor begins to speak his lies spew forth with amazing speed and are believed as if it were the truth. They preach fables just as God said they would and the many who listen to them will be deceived. All one needs to do is mix in a few Biblical truths into the sermon, add their own interpretations, stir in some jokes, smiles and helpful antidotes and out comes a honey-dripping porridge of lies.

If you can't hear the lies being told, then you have a serious problem. But remember, a pastor can say all the right things and still lie to you. How? By ignoring Biblical truths. Not preaching the whole Bible. Adding and taking away things in the Bible. Remaining silent to warn you of dangers, false teachings and failing to instruct his church members to go share the gospel to the lost.

These are just some of the tricks and lies pastors use to dupe those who dare listen to them. The more you listen to their sermons, the deeper you will fall into their web of lies.

IT IS TRUE or IS IT A LIE?

When they saw the inscription on the wall in the catacombs it said, "Obey your pastor, not Jesus." We then knew it was okay to disobey God and we did so.

Bible. Pastors want you to think you must belong to a pastor-controlled church to be saved. If you leave, you backslide. Jesus would rather that you go share the gospel to the poor and the slaves of sin than listen to another pastor's sermon that will not save the lost. Go then to your pastor's sermon and disobey the Lord. You know who your master is now!

May 19

If you keep ignoring the Lord's commands, He will abandon you. In fact, those who do disobey are not saved and therefore are not and never have been under the promise of salvation. If you have no heart to share eternal life with the lost, you are not His flock no matter what your pastor says otherwise. Get saved and you will save others. That's how the true Biblical church operates. It is God's method He uses to share the gospel.

May 20

Most pastors in churches are in fact unsaved pastors. This had to occur for the apostate churches to grow and thrive to create a falling away from the true gospel. This is what Jesus warned us about by following the blind, as both will fall into the pit. The danger is the unsaved pastor does not only spin fables in his sermons, he tells all the unsaved church members they are saved when they are not!

May 21

Silent elders in the church are wrongful and nonproductive and that includes every old believer in the church. They should be speaking, preaching, teaching in the pulpit how to reach the lost for Christ sharing their wisdom, but sadly pastors silence them, keeping them out of the pulpit and horrifically, these elders can't speak to teach as they have never shared the gospel to the lost. Thank the pastor for these works of darkness bearing no fruit.

May 22

Discipline is quick and severe upon those called by God to expose wrongdoing in the church. Pastors misuse authority to inflict punishment upon the watchmen blowing the horn of warning. This fear is used to control the flock

May 23

Did Jesus announce that the people should gather to him because he was to perform church services? No, but pastors do! Did Peter? No, but pastors do! Did any Apostle do this? No, but pastors do! Did Paul or any Disciple do this? No, but pastors do! Pastors have hi-jacked the church from meeting in homes and they "program" the events to control thought, word and deed. There is no such authority or directive in the Bible for any pastor to perform church services. Read it and see with open eyes.

May 24

Pastors are the enemy of Christ when they lead the children astray. No matter how fabulous their sermons or how gentle and loving they are, they are vicious wolves in sheep clothing devouring the flock. The Bible warns you about them, yet you fall for their sweet bait and become ensnared in their apostate trap.

May 25

Pastors that yell, holler and scream are putting on a show of false authority. Parents yell at children to inflict fear, respect, obedience, attention and dominance and pastors do this too to control the flock. They are bags of empty wind yelling to impress and mesmerize those who worship him. This behavior is not biblical in most all cases. The Bible severely scolds the hypocrite apostates by God's prophets, but pastors do not fit this role and yell only to gain authority and please the flock. Were the apostles known for their loud yelling?

May 26

Another strange and uncomfortable tactic is to see pastors work themselves into a frantic emotional state of mind where they begin loud obnoxious and rude snorting like a mad charging bull between breaths. Don't be fooled into thinking this is a holy spirit bursting out of the pastor. The real Holy Spirit of the Bible is pure actual power, not an emotional pastor preaching fables behind closed doors that is not the gospel. Pastors use many tricky tactics to fake-out the congregation. Snorting is not Biblical.

May 27

What kind of fruit God wants? Is it loyal church attendance? That's what pastors want, but God still wants the lost to be saved. It would be nice if both could occur, but it does not. The churchgoer does only the church attendance thing, not the witnessing thing. Want proof? Observe what they do after church services. They do not go sharing the gospel to the lost. They go home or out to play. And millions of Christians are openly disobeying the Lord. They only obey their pastor.

May 28

The apostate Christian is taught by apostate pastors to have absolutely no fear of the Lord. And that's why these pastor-followers do not obey the Lord's commands. They fear not the Lord. Pastors now step in to take the place of God making the flock fear and serve himself. These Christians obey their church with great fervor and without conscience openly disobey Jesus and the apostles commands in the Bible.

May 29

Pastors do not teach the whole counsel of God's Word. They refuse to do so as it will tempt their congregation to get rid of him. He will not warn the apostates thriving in his own church that God promises that he will not hear your prayers. He will laugh at your calamity says Proverbs 1:24-26. *"I will spew thee out of My mouth."* Rev 15-17. These are a few warnings apostate pastors refuse to teach. The people perish if they blindly follow their pastor and are deceived.

May 30

Has your pastor been teaching the flock how to be a "disciple" of Jesus Christ? It is doubtful he has and likely never will. This is just more evidence your pastor is misleading you. The New Testament mentions the word disciple 270 times! Just who is your pastor kidding? You! You must be a disciple of Christ or you are not a Christian. Read John 8:31. As you can see, your pastor has clearly blindfolded you to be his disciple!

May 31

Is God upset with apostate pastors? Let's hear what God has to say, *"Cursed be he that doeth the work of the Lord deceitfully..."*- Jeremiah 48:10.

Another Month Passed and 7 More to Go!

If you can't hear a pastor lie in the first three to five minutes into his sermon, you need ears to hear! Sometimes they don't lie every once in awhile to throw you off tract if you dare suspect them, but this honesty is actually a very rare event. Pastors lie even when holding the Bible in hand saying, "I preach the Word of God." They preach about things God cares not of. They preach not to save the lost. They preach not Jesus' commands. They preach not Jesus' warnings. They preach not how to witness. They preach not how to distribute gospel tracts. They preach not how to Glorify God. They preach not the whole counsel of truth. They preach not ... You got the idea. They leave out the true gospel and that is called preaching lies! And when he finishes, nobody cares to preach or share the gospel to the lost. Remember this!

THE SERMON

Pastors never gave "sermons" or "controlled a church" in the New Testament. Just because they all do today does not mean it is proper or Christian.

Did you know that St. Paul told you that you do not need a teacher? He said it so you would not be taken in by false teachers. You can learn from reading the Bible and from the Holy Spirit who will teach you all things. But today, people go to church and the pastor is lifted on up high in his lofty place above the congregation and they worship him, hear him and obey him. This is <u>not</u> church and it is <u>not</u> fellowshipping.

FELLOWSHIPPING

When people *"go to church"* they are being told they are *"fellowshipping"* with each other, but in reality the only fellowshipping taking place is the people admiring their pastor and they fellowshipping with him and him alone.

The New Testament says the fellowshipping was so mutual everyone got to speak to the assembly of people, not just one or a few select persons. Everybody participated and it was "informal" and nobody went to a church building!

True fellowshipping is the assembly of the saints so they can share and teach each other and not be controlled by a pastor like what is taking place today. In fact, pastors were to serve for *"free"* not be *"hirelings."* Paul was a tent maker, he did not take tithe money or a salary from the brethren! Read your Bible again! We are all being duped in these last days.

June 1

Should you continue to attend a church where apostates have invaded? The Bible "commands" you to get out. Read 2 Corinthians 6:14-17. As long as you keep disobeying the Lord's commands and continue to compromise, the Lord will give you up to the false beliefs. You will discover too late your pastor and teachers were lying to you because you shunned the Word of God. If you follow a pastor, denomination, faith or tradition you will not follow the Word of God.

June 2

The Bible never said for Christians to gather, meet or worship in a pastor's house fifty-two times a year, yet that is the expected requirement pastors have burdened the flock with for life. Yet you can be certain not once have these pastors enforced God's command to go share the gospel to the lost. How many sermons? None! Not one of fifty-two meetings. Some pastors may mention it briefly only to skip onto something more important to him. This is not God's will.

June 3

Have you distributed fifty-two gospel tracts this past year? If you say, "No" then you owe God a great service. You obeyed your pastor and chose not to obey Jesus. Your pastor demands you to attend his church each week, fifty-two times a year and you loyally obey him. You would not even leave "one" tract each week for Jesus. Follow the Lord, not your pastor. You owe God fifty-two tracts, and for each year of your negligence failing the Great Commission. Many will owe thousands. Pay up!

June 4

In reality it is horrible and inexcusable for a Christian to leave just one gospel tract per week. That is sheer laziness. You should be leaving six to a dozen each day. Let's say three a day can be distributed with no effort on your part. You just leave one wherever you go, three times a day. Easy to do! You would reach 1,095 people each year for Christ. That's more than the most dedicated and devout churchgoer could only dream of reaching for Christ in his entire lifetime! More than the average pastor too! You could be the biggest soul-winner in your entire church. Imagine that!

CHAPTER 6
STOP BELIEVING

You are blindly believing everything your pastor tells you and as a result you are following an intelligent blind man who is misinterpreting Holy Scripture. You need to read books and periodicals that dedicate to "Contend for the faith once delivered to the saints."

Any churchgoing Christian who is not subscribing to these fundamentalist Christian resources <u>is being deluded, deceived and fleeced by their pastor</u>. So much so, if you try to warn these deceived churchgoers they will strangely go to verbal battle to defend their church and pastor while as the same time call God a liar. Stop believing your church and dare to believe God's Word in His Bible. Let every man be a liar, and let God be true!

June 5

Do not obey your pastor when he tells you to go share your faith! No, go instead and share the gospel of the Kingdom of God in the KJV Bible. Your faith may be apostate and you don't know it. It is how the deceived go about deceiving others. It is how the cults and false religions thrive. You can't go wrong if you proclaim the true gospel of Jesus of Nazareth as depicted in the KJV Bible. In fact, Jesus told us to proclaim the gospel as He taught it, not to share our faith (that could be in error). Think about that.

June 6

Where in the Bible does it tell you to assemble together each week in the pastor's house? The Bible does not tell us we must adhere to such a demanding weekly schedule. Pastors have pulled the wool over the sheep again! Did you read, *The Lost Gospel of Luke and His Friends*?

June 7

Have you ever taken time to read the names of pastor-owned churches? Many names are outright blatant lies and abominations. Take notice of them and see if they even do or have what the church name implies. Church of God is in reality the Church of the Pastor because the pastor owns it. Evangelist Church is the Dead Church of Nobody Witnessing to the Lost. Temple of God Church is the Temple of the Pastor because God says he does not live in man-made building that pastors erect. Many have holy names, but are disobedient churches.

June 8

Imagine pastors teaching that it is okay to murder, to have abortions. It is okay to let unrepentant homosexuals into the church and it is okay for them to be elected to be bishops, etc. The Bible says homosexuals will not inherit eternal life, but pastors don't care, it's still okay with them. After all, it is "their" church! This is not hate speech; it is what the Bible proclaims. Pastors have gone hog wild into filthy doctrines creating abominable congregations.

June 9

What is your dream? To own an expensive dream home? Is it plenty of retirement income? Or is it to travel the country and then the world? You could do these things and storing wealth in heaven by saving the lost and sharing the gospel in all of your activities. Begin on your weekend activities and start leaving gospel tracts everywhere you go. Your primary focus in life must be God's agenda first; to proclaim the gospel to the lost. Then you will be used of God. Order your gospel tracts today! See the Resources section near the last page of this book.

June 10

Pastors looking like pagan thugs. Many strange pastors think nothing of having scraggly unkempt beards, ear-rings, go-tees, foomanchu's, long ponytails, gangster-like clothing, use questionable language, etc., and think nothing of it despite the Bible saying to avoid the appearance of evil. They say it helps the lost relate to them, yet many do not even evangelize or do so in a Biblical manner. Radical pastors are just plain rebellious.

June 11

Millions of churchgoers are listening to pastors each week and also buying their pastor's books, recordings and videos and of these millions after hearing the pastor's sermons are actually motivated to go out and share the gospel? Few to none! That's the bare fruitlessness of apostasy. Satan loves these pastors! Satan does not mind you attending church services and listening to what appears to be a gospel. He just does not want you to obey the gospel. Praise God and disobey! It's the insult Satan loves to see going on in his churches. A true disciple obeys the Lord's commands and shares the gospel to the lost wherever they go. They don't need a pastor's sermon to motivate them into disobeying God.

June 12

It's what they don't say that will deceive you. Don't you just love listening to pastor sermons? Most Christians do. They tickle the ear with great emotional glee to uplift you into another dimension of thought and mind, a twilight zone of fabulous proportions that are not Biblical, but you think it is. Pastors are highly skilled at performing great distortions and bending Biblical reasoning to trick you. Many are victimized and ultimately become addicted to the never-ending series of creative sermons. The more you hear, the more you must return for more.

June 13

The great apostles and disciples changed the world and were fully motivated without pastor sermons; they had the Word of God and the Holy Ghost to move them into action to save the lost and to do good works. You could too! Pastor sermons today produce absolute rotten fruit in comparison. If you obey the Lord, you will not need pastor sermons. You will be too busy doing God's work to be wasting time with fruitless sermons by pastors who care nothing about teaching you how to obey and serve Jesus or teach you how to go proclaim the gospel to the lost. Millions are being deceived by sermons given by apostate pastors that appear as dedicated servants of Jesus Christ. But not the Jesus of the Bible.

June 14

When your boss tells you to do something, you jump to it! Your pastor tells you to show up at his church and you obey him. Jesus tells you to share the gospel to the lost and you ignore him. Oh yes you do! Read the commands Jesus made and list each one you're not doing. The time is now to realign your loyalties. Now is your opportunity to hear, serve and obey your Savior, Lord, King and Master. Now who will you obey?

June 15

We have all been lied to. The best thing you can do for yourself is to believe the Lord when he warns you not to be deceived. Wake up! He means you! Many just can't fathom the thought that the pastor they so dearly know and love is the vicious wolf that inwardly despises you and takes you to hell. The Bible said the wolves will be from your own ranks. He will be as an angel of light and will devour the flock, not save it, but devour it utterly. And you think God's Word does not apply to you? You have been warned.

June 16

Motivational speeches are the modern sermons pastors love to perform.

It is the church of positive thinking and absolute apostasy. They quote the Bible in these sermons to add the appearance of legitimacy. Televised pastors are a perfect example. These sermons do not teach you how to obey Jesus. You don't learn how to reach the lost. What is the end result? The lost are not saved. There's no fruit for the Lord, just a stench remains of a decomposed gospel.

June 17

How about pastors and churchgoers wearing crosses? The cross or crucifix is not Biblical in the strong sense that the early Christians did not wear them! The Bible never tells us to wear or display them in church gatherings or in our homes. In fact, it is a cursed thing. It is an instrument of torture and the Bible says cursed be anyone hung on a tree. These objects are idols. They are visible objects of devotion and God condemns "all" idols, and he condemns those who have them and use them. You see many deeply unrepentant and unsaved sinful pagans wearing them as a fashionable statement and as a superstitious good luck charm. Pastors wear them and they should not! No idols means..."<u>No</u> <u>Idols</u>."

June 18

Your pastor enjoys teaching God's will for you, such as in John 13:35 where Jesus commands you to love one another. Pastors emphasize to love church members and other believers only. The truth is you are to love and care for all people and you don't hear the rest of what Jesus commands. Pastors dissect the gospel into visible and hidden sections. They preach the sections that they want to be visible to you and keep hidden much of the true gospel. God's true will for you is completely hidden from you eyes and ears. Read your KJV Bible.

CHECK OUT

Everything your pastor preaches in his sermons and see if anybody is going to go out and save the lost for Christ due to the subject matter he spoke of. You will find a pattern that his sermons do not equip the saints to do so. He is preaching a different Bible and a different Jesus, a different apostle, etc. He is very good at his deception!

EVER LEARNING

Have you noticed that Christians, mostly the churchgoers of course, are buying Christian books by the dozens. Buying pastor sermons on tapes and DVD's and attend church seminars, evangelistic conferences, you name it and yet they all have one nasty habit. What is that nasty habit?

They all disobey God with a passion! With all their learning and yearning they just don't get it. That it is their job to go save the lost, but nobody in leadership positions are teaching them how to do it. And, what is worse is they don't even want to learn how!

Sadly, this is the "fruit" of the modern day church. It's all about faithful church attendance, worship and no obedience to Christ. They only listen to and obey their pastor and that is the truth. You shall know them by their fruit and their fruit, in God's eyes, stinks rotten. Why? Because the lost are going to hell and that is the one thing, the one thing, God wants us to prevent and to stop, to go save the lost, go share the gospel, and it's the one thing churchgoing Christians don't want to do.

Something is awfully wrong in the churches if this is the sort of fruit it is producing. You need to come out of your church to go serve the living God, because He is not inside your church. He's not there! The Bible says so. He does not dwell in building made by man. Your pastor says otherwise. Who you going to believe? Who will you serve? Who will you obey? You can't serve two masters. Serve the Lord and leave your pastor behind in his church!

Books and more Books

THE PASTOR'S BRAIN

If you look closely you will see that God has made the pastor's brain different than the normal person. He has special powers to persuade people to give him their money and to convince them to listen to his sermons and to follow and to obey him without question. That is power!

These are amazing abilities. God has also made us subservient to the pastor and has told the pastor to go build church buildings and charge admission or attendance fees and to perform worship services inside the House of God. The pastor has been commissioned by God to build a physical temple and command all believers to come fellowship with the pastor on each Sabbath, which just so happens to be on Sunday, not Saturday and to collect tithe money too!

The pastor has a special brain and powers to magically make people believe anything his says is right with God. And you know, he is right. Because the God he serves is not the same God of the Bible. It's a counterfeit God.

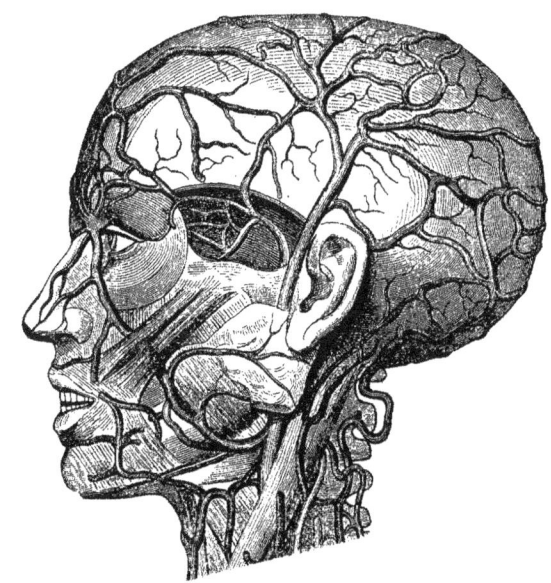

June 19

Read the paper; watch the crime on the news. Your pastor, like all pastors, does not teach that leaving gospel tracts around can in time decrease and stop crime. Shame on those pastors! A career criminal saved by a tract reduces crime and allows less to be victims of crime. One less drunk driver, one less murder, three less rapes, or dozens of robberies thwarted, etc. That's why you need to get your tracts out in great force. The murder you stop may be your very own! Your pastor does not care about crime prevention. If he did, he would be seeing to the Lord's business instead of church business that is enmity to God. What are you doing to stop the horrors of madness invading our land? There should be shame on all disobedient Christians for doing nothing to reach the lost for Jesus. You are the criminal in God's eye.

June 20

Did your pastor tell you to visit Christians in jail or in prison? When did he tell you to go? When? When did your pastor instruct you to go into town to proclaim the gospel? When did he go? All have chosen to disobey God. Why then do you call Him your Lord when you openly disobey Him? Most all churchgoers do not obey Him.

June 21

The larger the church the worse it will be. Jesus refers to his *"little flock"* in Luke 12:32 and he congratulates the Philadelphia church, which has little strength. Christians should think twice before joining a big church or huge denomination. Jesus said the path is narrow to heaven and *"few"* will find it. He said this as a warning.

June 22

Do not be duped by your pastor! You must perform good works as prescribed in the Bible on a daily basis. You must conform to God's ideals not your pastor's dreams, visions, desires and perspectives. The lost is to be saved by the faithful doing of your hands. You do not have a right or excuse to disobey the Lord or shun the Lord. You will sadly answer for your slothful laziness and uncaring heart for the things of God. The church is full and bursting at the seams with do-nothing pastor followers.

June 23

Listen closely to the lyrics church people sing and you will witness an abomination of singing lies to the Lord. How? They do not do what they say they are doing in the song. Many references are made in these songs that they will witness and shout loudly to proclaim God, but they don't and they sing it anyway. Apostasy, disrespect, lies and blasphemy is performed with the pastor's full blessing. Whatever you dare to sing to the Lord will be held fully accountable as a promise you must obey. Don't sing lies. Refuse to sing a verse in the song you know you will not keep. In hell is where liars shall dwell. Sing a truthful song to the Lord.

June 24

Christians do not see that Satan will use their church and family to stop you from serving the Lord. Church attendance never serves the Lord despite what your pastor demands you to believe. Serving the Lord is doing what God commands; He wants merciful action, not sacrifice and church attendance with lip service. Family, church, work time, personal activities, vacation time can all become idolatrous if you are not using these "times" and "activities" for the Lord. Your pastor should be teaching you how to obey the Lord's commands in relation to reaching out to share the gospel to the lost.

June 25

Here you will find the Lord Jesus explaining perfectly the typical church member today, 1 John 2:3-5. Go read it. You will see and read with wide open eyes the liars gleefully singing in the church with the amiable pastor assuring them they are saved, which is just another bold-face lie by a wool-covered wolf. It is time to go back and read what Jesus is saying. The truth will set you free. If you <u>want</u> to be set free.

June 26

If you are doing nothing to proclaim the gospel to the lost, you need to be reminded what Jesus said in John 15:1,4,5, *"...without me you can do nothing."* You're still doing nothing? That should tell you something!

June 27

Have you ever gone into a dark seedy bar room and left some gospel tracts like a secret agent working under cover for the Lord? Why not?

June 28

It is unchristian to proclaim the gospel to the lost. It is a sin to distribute gospel tracts. It is honorable to disregard God's commands to share the gospel. It is honorable to be seen in the church, but shameful to be seen witnessing in public places. Your pastor teaches well, as this is the way of the apostates. You know them by their fruit. 2 Peter 2:1-3.

June 29

If you are not a soul winner, go blame your pastor for not focusing on Christ's mission, purpose and agenda. Then blame yourself for being deceived because God warned in His Word *"do not be deceived,"* but you chose not to believe God. Read Acts 20:27-31.

June 30

You can claim Jesus as your savior, yet deny him as your Lord. That is one of the great secrets apostate pastors use to enslave the flock. A "form" of Godliness is cultivated with obedience to the pastor. If you are not daily sharing the gospel of the Lord with your own lips, feet and hands you are denying Jesus before men! Get out of that false church as fast as right now! Go and serve the Lord; alone if you must, but go!

Another Month Passed and 6 More to Go!

Have you noticed the antichrist pastor? He demands your loyalty to him and his church. Hand over your money and *"the man anointed by God"* will assure you are saved and going to heaven. He preaches "happy things" to cheer you up that you are a good servant to the Lord. He never demands you to go save the lost. He will never reject you (unless you expose him) so you won't reject him (Titus 3:10). It is too easy to be a churchgoing Christian and the pastor wants you to do nothing for the Lord

BEWARE OF VISITORS

When a pastor comes to your home, beware! He is after your money! He will often visit a new congregant of his church and with strange powers begin blessing your physical possessions, your property as if he was performing a Christian act. It sounds good. It looks good, but it is a scam.

Nowhere is this practice condoned in the Bible and pastors do not have *"special powers"* given to them by God. Wake up! Pastors are doing hundreds of non-biblical acts and nobody questions them. They are given freedom to do what they want to do.

to save the lost. He wants you to bring a friend to church to make him into a non-soul-winning church member. His church grows. It's all so easy! Matthew 23:15.

APOSTASY BOOKS YOU SHOULD READ

On my Web site I list many eye-opening books exposing false teachers in the church today. Many of the books we do not publish, but I have read them all. They truly are worthy of reading. The state of your soul is at stake!

There are dozens of apostasy related books. Have you wondered why your pastor is "very silent" about mentioning any of these books? Why is he not contending for the faith? You need to ask the tough and bold questions or you will be duped by a loving, soft-spoken pastor. The Bible calls them, "wolves in sheep clothing." Yes, they look just like sheep. Jesus also called them, "hirelings" and he warned you that if you permit yourself to be decieved you will be destroyed. Read the Bible, one more time!

CHECK OUT OUR FREE ARTICLES

My Web site has many free Christian articles and many articles of general interest to give you knowledge, wisdom and save you much grief. Knowledge is power. Visit: JamesRussellPublishing.com

NOT ALL PASTORS ARE BAD

Just because a pastor owns or operates out of a church building does not make him an apostate. It is just that most pastors today who own or hold worship services in church buildings are apostate. You really need to examine their teachings and see if they really are equipping the saints to minister and perform good works. Problem is, most are not doing what the church is ordained to perform according to the Bible.

Your best to start with the attitude that all churches and all pastors are apostate and let them "prove" to you that they are not. Most people believe otherwise in reverse then wonder how and why they became fooled. Remember Saint Paul congradulated those who challenged his teaching comparing his preaching to the Bible. You should too!

CHAPTER 7

SELFISH SERMONS

Listen to a pastor's sermon in church or on television. It feels good doesn't it? It is designed to be dripping honey and to be entertaining, but again, those who hear his voice will obey him, not Jesus. They will have no desire to go save the lost! That is the big test to see if a sermon is on target with God's will. Most sermons are selfish in nature. The hearer is hearing words that only pleases himself while the killing and raping goes on in society by those who are not saved. And you know what? They could care less!

July 1

What good is church attendance if the pastor teaches hypocritical doctrine? What good is church attendance if you are not being taught how to obey Jesus' commands? What good is church attendance if the lost are not being saved in your own city? What good is church attendance if God says you have worshipped Him in vain due to your lack of good works and obedience to Him? What good is church attendance if you end up in hell? Church attendance will never cover your sins and will never save you. The Bible says so! 2 Timothy 3:13.

July 2

Pastors are teaching, by silent omission, to disobey the command of Jesus to go bear much fruit for the Lord. To go save the lost, etc., read John 15:8. Pastors never warn with great Godly fear that Jesus "promises" the ultimate punishment for ignoring this command. If he does not find fruit, He breaks off the fruitless branch and destroys it with fire! Sounds like a description of hell and a stern warning to us all. This may be your last warning. Stop following your pastor. Get to work. Romans 16:17.

July 3

Why is it pastors do not lead their flock out of their church and instead have everyone meet downtown, so everyone can share the gospel with the lost? Share their testimonies to the lost? This would bring much glory to the Lord. Truly, pastors have confiscated the gospel and have no true heart's desire or intention to reach the lost. They care not of the fruit of the flock and all fall into the pit. 2 Corinthians 11:13-15.

July 4

Pastors who receive salaries are clearly hirelings Jesus warned of and are acting contrary to the command of the Lord. They are also bribed by churches and boards to teach what they want. Read Matthew 10:8-9. These pastors never walk by faith for God to supply their need; they have prostituted themselves for a fine paycheck. Do not be fooled by the hireling.

July 5

Most all pastor-owned churches have an unholy handshake with the world where they must dare not speak out against anything the government considers public policy. If disobeyed, the pastor loses his tax-exempt status. Not losing his church mind you, he just has to now pay income taxes like the common people! Get away from these compromising pastors. They will not preach the truth or warn the flock of danger. They have denied the Word of God to fill their own bellies with man's manna.

July 6

Just when you thought it could not get any worse most all pastors and denominations now have written agreements to obtain government money. If certain things in the Bible are taught, the pastor will go to prison and church property confiscated. Sermons are to be government approved! You should read the IRS rules your pastor has agreed to obey and in so doing deny Christ. You should be meeting in individual homes, not in church buildings, just like the early church did, successfully. You need to get out of these unclean churches. Is your church one of the unfaithful? It likely is.

July 7

Did you know your pastor was giving money loans to certain church members? Did you know he too was getting loans while you had to take out your mortgage with oppressive banks? These corrupt deals are commonplace and you did not know that your pastor hid them from your eyes. What else is he hiding from you? He is hiding much of the Word of God. You can be sure of that.

July 8

Who gave pastors the authority and power to bless homes, motorcycles, cars, property and people? Did Jesus go about blessing everything he saw? Did the apostles do likewise? No. Then why is your pastor doing these unbiblical things? He wants you to believe that he is a special holy person with mystical power whom God will obey his commands. Beware of such witchcraft! Get far away from these "blessing pastors." 1 Tim.4:1.

July 9

Did you know that only pastors are doing the baptizing? But the Bible never gave pastors the sole authority to do this? See how they muscle in dominating and taking over everything in the church? The Bible never says only pastors can baptize. You can do it too.

July 10

When will you get off of your lazy rump and oder some gospel tracts? When? If you do not do so right now you will never do it. Now is the time to act. Contact our Web site for listings of companies that print gospel tracts. Check out FEASITE.org as they also have some fabulous tracts that expose apostasy and will set you right with God. Jesus said if you do not gather you scatter and become his enemy. Believe what he says and do it what he says. Stop obeying your pastor and obey the Lord!

Now that over six months has passed, think of all you read here so far and still your pastor is silent on these issues, intentionally side-stepping them. There is no excuse for pastors to be ignoring God's commands and warnings and to be manipulating their flocks. We still have six months to go!

July 11

Why is it when you go to church you do not see anybody on fire for the Lord? I mean, you don't see anybody urging others to go out and save the lost. It's like a sinful thing for it to be mentioned at all in church. Nobody talks about it among each other. A sermon here and there and rare. How come you do not leave gospel tracts everywhere you go? What sort of fruit is being harvested that the Lord approves of is taking place? Did He even tell you all to go to church each week? No. But he did tell you all to go save the lost. What is really going on inside your church?

July 12

Pastors should be teaching you to be an evangelist and others. How many are in your church actually and visually can be seen reaching the lost? Where do they go? To special assigned places? Can they be found where the sinners are? Do you distribute gospel tracts?

July 13

Yes, your pastor is saving the lost after all. He is saving his lost church membership a firery place in Hell fire.

July 14

"If Christ were here now there is one thing he would not be - a Christian." - Mark Twain. That should tell you just how badly this apostasy thing has become and it is even much worse today than a hundred years ago.

July 15

"When a pastor muscles in and takes over a church he will paralyze human thought and twist the Bible's true meanings to serve himself to such an extent the poor sheep are spiritually and financially sheared by this minister of light. Remarkably, this flock will bleat loudly for mercy of deliverance upon anyone who approaches to warn them of danger. They serve their pastor, not Jesus. This is the worldly state of the established church system. The Bible calls it the Synagog of Satan. The deceived call it Christ's Church." - James Russell.

July 16

Pastors teach that faith keeps you safe, but the Bible screams that faith without works is dead, dead, dead. So, a living faith given by God produces much good fruit and this is considered good works and the Bible shouts loudly you will be judged by your works. Pastors refrain from telling sheep that sharing the gospel to the lost is the fruit Jesus is looking for, not church attendance with rebels, apostate pastors and disobedient children whom God calls bastards. Separate from them. God commands you to do so.

July 17

Tracts work to save the lost. Why? They contain the very Word of God. It is a surefire method to get the gospel out of the pastor-confiscated churches and into the world where it was meant to be used to perform the Great Commission. Get your gospel tracts and go bear much good fruit for the Lord. Go, go, go! Time is of the essence! This will be your first act of disobedience to your pastor, but a blessing to those you save from death.

July 18

The dead are in the churches. They do not obey the Lord to share the gospel. No good fruit. They are wonderfully nice people who don't give a damn for the damned (sinners). So they reap what they sow.

July 19

The only evangelism a pastor will do heartily and with great fanfare is to "recruit" new church members. He has no other true interest than the self-centered growth of his church and he will focus his target to the "well-to-do" in his secret marketing plan. Making money drives his desire and a prosperous ministry his motivation, but this he will disguise with a false presentation filled with lying wonders. Jesus came to preach the Good News to the poor.

July 20

God's blessings be poured out upon all faithful servants who go out every day without pay to share the gospel with the lost. They will shine like bright stars.

July 21

Too many chiefs, too few Indians! There are multitudes of pastors, but few are true followers of the Lord. There are woefully too few willing to sow God's Word to reap a harvest. The pastors angrily stomp their feet at the thought of teaching Godly ministry technique to the flock for the purpose to go into the world and share God's Word to the bad sinners in their own city. The chief cares not for the lost and he cares not for the Indians and he cares not to share the Kingdom of God.

July 22

Pastors dazzle the flock with admirably talented oratory skills. The sheep become mesmerized. The Bible says they are "bewitched" by these false teachers, but the flock cannot grasp the concept that Satan roars as a lion inside churches. The Bible warns that it will be pastors - those who teach the flock and the hirelings - who are the devil's disciples that will devour the flock. But not my church, they cry, God lies. God warned, and they turned away from His warning.

July 23

The apostate will never defend God's Word. They will only defend their faith, belief, tradition, denominational doctrine and their leaders. They will boldly stand against God's Holy Word with incredible stiff-neck stubbornness. They got this way from listening to their trusted pastor instead of hearing Jesus' Word in the KJV Bible. Remember this! Don't let this happen to you. If you must leave your church to walk with the Lord, then do it!

July 24

What is the history of your church denomination? Does it involve bloodshed? Or torture? How about prophesies that never came true? Beginnings established upon tradition or factual historic truth? You must examine the foundation to see if that denomination was and still is unbiblical, false, cruel or hateful. Yes, they do exist.

July 25

Pastors are not authorized to be collecting and hoarding the flock's tithe money. Giving money to a church or denomination is not Biblical, and they misappropriate the money to build buildings and make real estate and stock market investments. The needy Christian never sees a dime, but the early church used money collections to build no churches! The money was distributed back to the flock and to evangelize. Any other misuse is unbiblical, but most all pastors could care less.

July 26

The modern day churchgoer wants all the blessings from God, but they will not share the blessing or share God's knowledge or God's gospel to the lost whom desperately need God's Word to obtain blessings. Like thieves, the pastor never teaches how to perform your own ministry. He has his money-grabbing ministry and wishes you do not invest in God's work, the work you should be doing... to bless others!

July 27

The role of the Watchman is to give stern warning, like a lighthouse near the coast, to avoid shipwrecked souls. This duty is the responsibility of all true believers. Some loud-spoken pastors assume the role of a watchman to fool the flock into believing they have special calling from God. These pastors can never be seen witnessing to save the lost beyond church property. In reality, the pastor should be teaching you how to be a watchman, contending for the faith once delivered to the saints. How come pastors are hijacking these duties from the saints? Ezekiel 3:17.

July 28

The next time you go out, look at everyone you see. Imagine that each person you see is going to hell. They very well may be! Christians should be busy sharing the gospel with great fervor and urgency, but they don't. Your pastor may not care, but Jesus, the Master, said this. *"...but he that believeth not is condemned already, because he hath not believed in the name of the only begotten Son of God."* John 3:14-18. If they do not believe then they are absolutely going to hell. What are you doing to save these people? Jesus came to seek that which is lost. So should you.

July 29

If your pastor refuses to preach, teach, instruct and "lead by example" and how the entire flock must evangelize, then shake the dust from your feet and abandon him. That's what the Bible tells you to do. You are to obey the Lord and do what He commands and go win souls for Him. You are not to remain in any apostate church. 2 Corinthians 6:14-18.

July 30

Take a walk on your lunch break and look around to see if you can find any gospel tracts. None, right? But how many churchgoers have passed by in the last twenty-four hours? There are dozens, hundreds, and even thousands in high traffic areas. Not one gospel message to be found? Now you know pastors are producing foul fruit when churchgoers care not to share, spread and proclaim the gospel to the lost. This is also your opportunity to stand in the gap and do the job, what professing Christians refuse to do. Not even a pastor will be found to help you! You will work alone, but you will be obeying your Master Jesus of Nazareth.

July 31

Pastors can not be found except in their church. Jesus was found traveling where the lost are and he was speaking, interacting, being involved with the lost. He was not playing church. Compare the two!

NOTICE THE TREE

Your pastor permits the decorations of trees inside his church and outside his church, yet he knows full well the Lord his God commands His people not to have any idols and specifically not to decorate trees as the pagans do.

This is just another example of outright disobedience and defiance against God. And guess what? He's got you doing it too!

The spirit of Santa (it spells, Satan) is alive inside your church.

Perhaps the Protestants should ask the nuns to pray for them. After all, it is only a matter of time the Protestants will be Roman Catholics. They are having many wonderful ecumenical meetings and gaining audiences with the pope. That one world religion is just around the corner now as the Bible is trashed and ignored.

CHAPTER 8

I will sing unto the Lord, but I refuse to obey Him! That is the song Christians sing inside their churches and they don't even realize that their song is nothing but noise to God's ears. He desires obedience over sacrifice. He said so! Jesus warned when he said, "Why call ye me Lord, Lord, and do not the things which I say?" Luke 6:46. Answer Him! Answer the question!

August 1

According to the Bible, if you do not preach the Word your faith is dead. James, the brother of Jesus, said it and that means you have to go preach the Word of God. But to whom do you preach? Do you preach to the lost? James said you must be an evangelist. That's right, he is speaking to you! He was not speaking to pastors. Just because pastors have stolen the Word for themselves, does not mean you are excused from your responsibility to go preach the word. If you do not gather you scatter.

August 2

Christians today do not even read the Word of God to establish a solid foundation for their faith. The result is they have a false and "different" faith and they learn it from apostate pastors. Sadly that is how cults and "big denominational religions" operate today to proclaim a partially true, yet still a false, gospel. You too will be deceived if you do not read and properly interpret the Word of God. Visit: FEASite.org

August 3

Apostate churches are masters at deceiving their church members. They have cleverly dissected the Word to bend its meanings into conforming to their beliefs and thereby fool the multitudes. Then they elevate the pastor to an unbiblical priest-like status to gain the admiration and devotion of the flock. Result? The flock believes in their church more than they believe in the Lord. It is a marvelous deception from the father of lies. Visit: PeopleOfTheLivingGod.org

August 4

Paul mentions some words you do not hear from the lips of pastors. Sermons do not mention the word peddle, in vain, distort, deception, etc. These are horrible words and a good pastor would not use them to expose apostasy. Why? He would be exposing himself. There are hundreds of words missing from your pastor's sermons. Find out why! Visit: James-RussellPublishing.com and the Christian links page!

August 5

Beware of the loving, kind, smiling, friendly pastor because it is these wonderful men in perfect disguise set to fool you. They are wicked sheep that are dressed in a finely woven coat of deception, but are vicious wolves to get you to worship God, but not to obey God. Wolves are heartless predators Satan uses to decimate multitudes of believers.

August 6

If you are not bearing "much" good fruit for the Lord you are not Jesus' disciple and that means you are none of his, no matter what church or what your pastor say's otherwise. Jesus is King. Read John 15:8. This means you must produce a lot of fruit! Also, attending church services does not produce fruit, so you had better face the truth now and serve the Lord and go proclaim the gospel just as Jesus told you to do and stop believing and obeying everything your pastor tells you.

August 7

Where is your devotion? Most all churchgoer's devotion is to their pastor. They truly and really do adore and worship him! They obey him with absolute trustful obedience. They even believe they are born again because their pastor told them so. The Lord demands loyalty to Himself. He will not share his Glory with your pastor, church or denomination.

August 8

What is your faith? Something you were born into, like growing up in a certain denomination? Most of us were, but we all must stop and question if our religion really is a true religion!

August 9

It should not surprise you to see the divorce rate in the "pastor controlled" churches as high as is in the pagan society. It's just another example of bad fruit and it is screaming loudly "something's awfully wrong." It is the false teaching and false leading of apostate pastors not feeding the flock with the "whole counsel of God." Many church member families are victimized and destroyed by these "love only" preaching pastors. They also need to preach the penalties of disobeying God's instructions. Example; do not be unequally yoked with unbelievers, do not associate with pagans, do not be entangled with unbiblical relationships, etc. Many churchgoers are not even authentic Christians! No wonder divorce is embarrassing the church.

August 10

Remember when you choose to disobey Jesus of Nazareth commands you are in open rebellion towards the Lord your God. That is so serious you may as well stop going to church because you are wasting your time. Even your worship is an annoying noise to God's ears! The Israelites chose to disobey God and God took away His promise to enter the Promised Land. All (millions) perished and only Joshua and Caleb entered with a more obedient generation. Keep obeying your pastor and disobey your Jesus and you will not enter the Lord's rest.

August 11

Are you a witch? The Bible says you are! That is, if you are the typical churchgoer and do not proclaim the gospel to the lost, you are guilty of witchcraft. The churches are full of unholy witches, male and female, and the chief warlock is the controlling pastor running the witches haven. Those who consistently choose to rebel against performing the commands of Jesus Christ is guilty of sin. Rebellion is of the sin of witchcraft. Your pastor should have taught you this long ago. Now you know all is not as well as your pastor wants you to believe. Obey the Lord.

August 12

The Bible is not just a big love story that is being taught by deceitful pastors, it is a very huge "book of warning." Most pages warn of God's retaliation for disobedience.

August 13

Remember when God took fearful action against apostates in the Bible? God had the earth swallow people alive or just drop dead. Since God does not do such dramatic action as a routine, people and pastors now

HE HAD TO CHOOSE HIS CHURCH OR HIS BIBLE

He who obeys his pastor cheats himself and denies the Lord Jesus by his very actions of disobedience to God's will. Many men refuse to choose to do what Jesus said to do, yet willingly and blindly obey their pastor's demands.

<u>One example</u>: Jesus say's to go save the lost, but 99.999% of churchgoing Christians won't be caught dead distributing gospel tracts, but you see them in church obeying their pastor's demand to "attend church" each week!

YOU ARE RESPONSIBLE

And who is it expected to go into the world to share the gospel to the lost? **You**!

And who is responsible for producing much good works and good fruit for the Lord? **You**!

And who is required to save the lost or that lost person's blood is upon your hands? **You**!

And who is to obey the Lord's commands? **You**!

And who is to read the gospel of St. James and stop becoming a hearer of the word, but become a doer of the Word of God? **You**!

And because your pastor and your church fold do choose to disobey their Lord's commands, who will pay the price for not saving the lost? **You**!

get away with open disobedience without fear of the Lord. But, your pastor does not tell you God will never be mocked and that God changes not. He has a different method to punish apostates. He has already answered them. He no longer hears their prayers! He gives them up to believing lies and fables pastors love to preach and ultimately Hell fire.

August 14

There is not one command in the Bible for pastors to preach to the flock. Not one! They are told to feed the flock with the Word, the "whole" counsel of God. That they do not do. Not even "sermons" are commanded to be performed by pastors. Now that pastors have taken on an unbiblical act of preaching sermons they have created clever speeches and have become the main attraction. People go to church to hear sermons, and they don't even assemble together to fellowship with the people in the adjacent pew! Now that's how pastors have taken 100% control of Christians to feed them fanciful lies with misleading and deceitful fables.

August 15

Churches are controlled today by incompetent and untrustworthy pastors who are not properly ordained by God to teach God's Word. Many are eloquent speakers with doctorate degrees, but these educated slick-talking frauds refuse to teach their sheep how to win souls for Christ. They teach how to get things from God, get the blessings, but they are blessed by your money donations.

August 16

The Bible gives no example of a minister or pastor to go from one church to another to collect money for his ministry. Did not God say in his Word He would supply every need? These traveling ministers are fly-by-night scam artists making you believe that if you give them money, they will go on your behalf to minister. Minister to whom? You won't find them on the streets sharing the gospel. They earn a living going to the apostate pastors who let these wolves in to steal God's tithe money! You would be way better off buying Bible tracts and distributing them yourself.

August 17

Churches have become targets of con-artist-traveling ministers to entertain, tell sad stories and perform every other gimmick to get you to open your wallet to the Lord. In return you will be blessed. In reality you are cursed. God does not bribe and He already promises blessings to those who obey Him. Pastors love to see you being entertained, while outside the church the lost cries can't be heard. Loud religious music drowns out the gunfire, the screams and the horror. You leave feeling you have served God. You got what you bargained for.

August 18

Any hypnotist can tell you that pastors are using hypnotic devices to get you to believe and obey him. This is one of the bewitching powers given to pastors by Satan. Watch out for any pastor telling you what to say or when to sit down or when to applaud or when to praise God. These are reinforcing "subconscious suggestion command" tactics to control your mind into deeper states of hypnosis. Television ministers do it too. This hypnosis is real and your pastor is using it upon you despite your disbelief.

August 19

You can't serve two masters. Jesus said so. You serve the one you routinely obey. Sadly, pastors teach that by serving the church you are serving the Lord. Not according to your Bible! Never is a command given in the Bible to serve the church or to tend to the needs of a pastor. You must serve the Lord's needs and desires by doing what He said to do in His Word. Are you reachingt out to save the lost each day? Each week?

August 20

God was concerned for you and He used somebody to send His gospel to save you, yet you have no such loving concern for others who are lost, so God can't send or use you to be a blessing. Is that how you repay Him? Pastors teach this exact thing by their intentional silence on such matters. You will not even be merciful. No mercy for the lost! Jesus warns if you do not bear fruit you will be cut off. The time is now to disobey your pastor and go save the lost.

August 21

When your eyes and ears have been opened by God, you will no longer trust pastors or listen to their sermons of blasphemy. You will see through their tactics when you realize that when all is said and done, all who listened still won't go proclaim the gospel to the lost! All still choose to disobey God's commands. Nothing changed, except your money was magically transferred to the pastor. A miracle has just happened! Even Jesus can't get them to buy a gospel tract to save the lost!

August 22

Christians today are Biblically illiterate. Are believers ignorant of the Bible? Yes, they are. Blame the pastors. They do the teaching! They won't even teach the Word of God for fear of offending the flock. The churchgoer craves false Biblical interpretation of knowledge as given by confidence men (con-artist pastors) and yet he despises God's true Biblical knowledge.

August 23

Pastors point to Bible verses in their sermons and churchgoers flip the pages obediently seeing the truth, but the pastor just implanted another damaging lie into their heart and mind! False interpretation of the Word of God is nothing but a lie and a lie can never be truth, unless you choose to believe a lie, then the lie becomes your truth! People just can't believe a good man of the cloth could boldly lie in church. They do it all of the time.

August 24

Churchgoers all have a disease called apathy. They care not for the lost. They care not to bring glory to God with service of good works that He desires. They are "indifferent" to God's agenda. They are "church addicts" hooked on the pastor's bewitching sermons. Religious zombies.

August 25

The faith of our fathers has changed so drastically from the New Testament and teachings of Jesus Christ to the modern day church that pastor sermons and their doctrine can no longer be recognized as truly being Christian. What they teach are heresies cloaked as being Biblical. One needs only to read the Bible to see it.

August 26

The new counterfeit gospel devised by apostate pastors is designed to guide the people along social and economic themes. Saving the lost does not "fit in" with this ideal, so pastors just ignore what Jesus wants and then continue to preach how you can get things from God. Give money to the pastor to support more of this nonsense? Many do.

August 27

Church programs are centered on recreation and emotion. Even listening to pastor sermons is wonderfully entertaining! It is another brainwashing program to get you away from the real true gospel. Apostasy is not outside the church, it is residing in deep places inside the church. The severest attack on the true Word of God comes from inside the church by the pastor himself. Change the Word of God just a tiny bit and you now have doctrines of demons!

August 28

We all must continue steadfastly in the apostles' doctrine - Acts 2:42. This is a key to remaining true to the Lord. It will also open your eyes to the great apostasy deceiving millions, actually billions of churchgoers. It is the foundation of Christianity. Deviation is simply a false gospel. Scripture is everything! 2 Timothy 3:16. Your compass and chart is the KJV Bible.

August 29

When you read the Bible with an open heart and teachable spirit, it will step on your toes causing you pain. You will scream in righteous anger when you discover your pastor deceived you. Millions of people are being deceived by pastors just in one major denomination alone! Millions more in other denominations are victim. Satan can blind you. He has that power and he is using it in his churches. Are you a member of his church?

August 30

Are you true to the Lord? Most say they are, but when they pick up and read the Bible, they will see their false ways and discover the Pharisees still exist in their own church misleading the flock with lies built upon more lies. So many lies it boggles the mind as to how the church pulled it off. If you tell a lie often enough, it is "perceived" to be true, but it is still a lie.

August 31

Let us build the Kingdom of God on earth! Will you join us? Let us pray. Please join hands and work with the church to bring this wonderful gospel to all mankind. Sounds good? Well, it is a lie. A different gospel is being preached. God never told Christians to build the Kingdom of God.

YOUR BLESSING

Have you noticed in pastor sermons when they talk about God giving wealth that the pastor never says you can start your own ministry? You have to open your ears to hear what the pastor does not say to discern his sermons.

He will get everyone to cheer when he uses Biblical passages to convey wealth upon the flock, but what will they do with the money that comes to them? I will tell you they will selfishly spend it on themselves and give huge chunks of to their pastor or to their church, but they will not use it or invest it into their own ministry to save the lost. No, the lost will not be saved!

NO MORE TITHES

You will certainly prosper when you stop giving your tithe money to apostate churches and dishonest pastors who are only taking God's money and not using it for His glory and not saving those who are lost.

Take your ex-tithe money and now invest it directly in your own ministry and use the money to pay your bills associated with your ministry.

I want you to question your pastor's wisdom... how come he never preaches a sermon telling his flock how they should go form their own ministries? Have you noticed how "his ministry" take precedence over everyone? It's not Biblical what he is doing. The Bible does not even authorize him to build a church building, yet he does so with impunity.

When you begin your studies of apostate churches you will see a lot of things pastors are doing that are not Biblical. They do what they want to do with "no accountability to anybody" not even to God. They will cheat God out of His tithe money and cheat you out of having your own ministry as God wants you to have. We all must go forth and bear good fruit and save the lost.

CHAPTER 9

IN THE HIGH PLACES

Have you ever wondered why the pastor elevates himself or positions himself so that he is the center of attention and placed in a position of dominance over the flock? It's the same old trick Satan used when he wanted to sit in the high place in the sides of the North above God.

Pastors are placing themselves between people and God and become the "idol shepherd" and the people no longer hear or obey Jesus, but rather they hear and obey their pastor.

September 1

What is the mission of God? It is to preach the Word of God to win men to Jesus Christ? Not behind closed doors inside your church, but to do this in public places where the lost are to be found. Read your Bible and then get to work. Your pastor should be preaching sermons on how you can accomplish God's mission instead of his own agenda.

September 2

Apostasy will take you by complete surprise. You won't be able to see it coming. It grabs you like a snake without mercy and slowly squeezes God's true Word out. It replaces the true gospel with a similar, but very different gospel. It even replaces Jesus of Nazareth with a sin-loving version that is tolerant of sin, ordains homosexuals, and requires no repentance or good works. It's the type of gospel being preached in Christian churches. Some more extreme than others but they all preach a "different" gospel, a "different" Jesus. The Great Falling Away has arrived!

September 3

Luke is the book in the New Testament that deals almost exclusively with apostasy. Saint James and Saint Paul too. You will notice that pastors totally avoid quoting any verses from Luke. They don't want you to go read the gospel of Luke, James and portions of Paul's writings as it will expose their wrongdoing. But, every book in the Bible has something to say about apostasy, if you will only read it, it will set you free from bondage! That is a wonderful gift from God.

September 4

Be very carefull when a pastor teaches that, *"once saved always saved"* doctrine. If it were true, then Jesus and his apostles wasted their warnings that the faithful could be deceived and fall away. Those warnings are numerous and not to be ignored. Your pastor is wrong to dismiss Biblical warnings or try to explain they do not apply to you. They apply to all of us! The roaring lion is not just seeking to devour the lost, he has Christians targeted as prey. Read all of the warnings in the Bible. Learn to fear God. This is totally lacking in churches today.

September 5

Pastors have not only hijacked the Bible, they have elevated themselves into positions of strong authority to rule over the flock. God did not authorize or appoint pastors to elevate themselves to positions of power and control. You can't find it in the Bible. They even take tithe money when there is no temple! Go read Luke 18:14 and Matthew 23:4-12. Beware of the leaven of the pastors.

September 6

Churchgoers have an unbiblical teachable spirit that permits them to learn from what their pastor says, and "crave" for more, but they are also possessed by an evil dumb spirit to stop them from learning and obeying God's Word. They reject God for a man. Church today is that dangerous!

September 7

God's will comes first. He wants and commands you to share the gospel to the lost over and above your desires and daily cares. You must put His Kingdom first and not your own. Luke 14:26. If you keep on ignoring God's commands, you will not escape His wrath. God will not tolerate disobedience you can be sure of that. Fear Him, not your pastor.

September 8

The need for faithful witness is needed now more than ever. The great mission field is not in the jungles, it is inside the church buildings and the homes and streets in Christian communities! One easy way to witness is to write a gospel verse on a dollar bill and let it circulate to hundreds of thousands of people. According to the Secret Service in the USA it is not defacing money for the money is not rendered unspendable. You could write this in the white border area. But don't expect your pastor to give you such ideas because he has absolutely no plan or interest to share the gospel with anybody outside of his church membership. It is sad, yet true.

September 9

Each week in church the pastor-worshipping church member profess to know God, but by their deeds they deny HIm. Titus 1:16 says this is true and it is true. Just look around inside your church and you will see the fruit your pastor is blooming on his tree. They are taught assurance of salvation is proof of their faith, but hold to this false doctrine for safety and comfort. They are taught if you doubt your salvation you doubt God's Word, but there is no evidence of fruit with obedience to the Word (John 8:31). Also read II Cor. 13:5.

September 10

You can't save the lost if you are lost. That should tell you what shape you are in in God's eyes. You may look fine in your pastor's eyes, but if you are not on fire to share the gospel you are worthless dung. God say's so and your pastor should be teaching you these things!

September 11

Your pastor teaches you are saved, but you are headed for eternal damnation. A fruitless barnch is cut off. You love those babbling sermons, but you have already backslided. Go read 2 Timothy 2:15 and 4:1-5.

September 12

When you see the begging homeless, do you give them a gospel tract when they beg for spare change? Give God's word along with your donation. Or do you ignore the poor and give nothing? Be truthful. Are you always invoking Proverbs to justify not giving to the poor that a man whom does not work shall not eat? While this is true, you should also be merciful, as much as you should. Give when you feel the Lord would approve of your act of mercy. At the very least, the homeless are the lost and you can reach them with a gospel tract.

September 13

"Blessed are they that hear the Word of God, and keep it." Luke 11:27. Your pastor's sermons are not the Word of God. He may inject God's Word into his tall entertaining stories to make you believe God is using him to proclaim God's Word, but do not be fooled. God already said what He wanted to say and it is in the KJV Bible. Hear God's Word and read God's Word and keep it. Obey it. Do it! Perform your faith!

September 14

Do not be ashamed to discover you are apostate. Join the club. Many in the Bible were, but turned their face to hear and serve the Lord. Saint Paul was apostate. So was I, and still I must watch out to not fall into it again. Apostate pastors are masters of deception. Just listening to them will fool you. Don't let pride stop you from repenting of your error. We make mistakes. Ask God to save you from false shepherds and He will.

September 15

The Bible does say you should hear the Word of God. Pastors love to pound this hard into your ears, not because it is Biblical, but to fool you into believing hearing the Word is ordained more than any other means. It makes you a "captive" audience enslaved to listen to and hear the pastor, like an addiction. He does not tell you there was no New Testament Bible in the early church and reading just was not possible, but hearing was. Today we have the written Word. More reading of the Bible and less hearing of pastor stories and fables is needed.

September 16

Abortion- The one who causes the fruit (unborn baby) to depart from the pregnant woman is to be killed. The Lord views abortion as murder. Exodus 21:22-25. Also read the 6th Commandment *"Thou shalt not kill."* God is not silent on this abortion holocaust. People also sacrificed babies to a demon named Baal and really bad things happened to those who did.

September 17

Most despised and ignored is the Biblical command to separate from apostate churches, pastors, denominations, etc. Deut. 22:9-11. God never accepts the mixing of error with His truth. John 17:17. He is very serious about this. You are commanded to depart from false teachers and not bid them farewell or you will partake in their sin. Imagine the wrath of God upon those who choose to ignore God's commands and stubbornly remain in apostate churches! Read 2 John 1:8.

September 18

Choose the Lord and His way. Adam and Eve chose to ignore God's warning (Genesis 2:15-17) and Christians still ignore God's warnings today. They disregard God's commands to rather obey their pastor. They dare not skip church attendance, not even to go save the lost! Obey the pastor. Fear the pastor. Serve the pastor. To hell with the lost, let's go to church! Too bad they could not do both; attend saintly assembly and save the lost. Pastors allow neither.

September 19

Israel lost blessings due to disobedience and the Lord Himself said so. Read Zechariah 7:1-14. He changed not. You will lose blessings if you keep ignoring His Word telling you to "perform" good works, etc. Titus 2:14

September 20

If you think these warnings are harsh, do not blame the author. Send your complaints, grumbling, murmuring to God, if you so dare. God is warning you in His Word. That's way more than your pastor is doing! If you turn from the Lord now, you may never be able to return. You can fall, you can be cut off. God's Word says so despite your pastor saying otherwise. The Lord will not be mocked. You will reap a bill to pay in an eternity in hell. God said so. Just read the Bible.

September 21

Christians have "no sense of urgency" to save the lost. Worse, they don't have any desire to grab gospel tracts and plaster the town with God's Word. They just don't care. They certainly won't preach on a street corner. Yet it takes no skill and requires so little effort to leave tracts and still they refuse to *"do the Lord's business."* They're too preoccupied begging God for more blessings and too busy tending to church activities. They wait for their pastor to show them how to do God's will, yet they find no urgency for such foolish matters as saving the lost when planning to build a new church, etc.

September 22

Beware! Pastors that boldly state that their church houses the Lord are fooling you. The Lord does not dwell in buildings made by men. These pastors will manipulate you into believing their church is the house of God. Nonsense! The Bible itself, even more so the New Testament, reveals Christians never built a church to house God. Stop being duped by these deceiving pastors! Read your Bible!

September 23

Trusting your pastor will send you to hell. The Bible warns repeatedly to trust not in man, but to trust in God alone. You are being warned again. This may even be your last warning. It is time to read the KJV Bible. You can find the answers there to set you free! A pastor lies for a dollar when he could earn $1.50 telling the truth. Go figure!

September 24

If you listen to pastor sermons and still find that you are not going out sharing the gospel with the lost, you are under the pastor's bewitching spell. Sermon-hearing is not bearing fruit and is not good instruction and it is poor teaching, if you are not motivated to obey the Lord's commands to share the gospel on a daily basis. You have a dead faith, which is the same form of Godliness your pastor has. A false counterfeit faith!

September 25

Jesus is Lord, not your pastor! You would think this would be obvious, but on the contrary most churchgoers blindly obey their pastor and openly and grossly disobey Jesus words, instructions, commands and warnings. Truly, the pastor is their lord and savior and that is just one more reason such apostates are cut from the vine and will be burned in the fire. Jesus is Lord. Obey Him! I John 5:3.

September 26

In the Bible the voice from heaven did not say, listen to my pastor's sermons. The voice of your Father said to listen to Jesus, his Son. That command is direly needed today as churchgoers gather to listen endlessly to pastor sermons, much of which is full of fable-ridden stories, poor advice and instruction on how to keep disobeying God's Word. Amazing!

September 27

Obey Jesus, not your pastor! Why do you show up to church each week? You show up because your pastor said so. Why do you disobey Jesus command to go proclaim the gospel? That is because Jesus said so. Put 2+2 together. Who are you really serving? Go save the lost and let the dead remain in their churches. The Lord wills it. He told a man to do just that in the Bible.

September 28

You do not need to be a church member to be Christ's disciple. Heresy you say? Then you proclaim Jesus to also be a heretic. He rebuked his apostles for wanting to stop a man from doing the Lord's work. That man was not an apostle and nobody knew him or ordained him, but Jesus fully accepted him and his work. There is your perfect example and your opportunity to break out of the do-nothing church crowd and go alone if need be to serve and obey Jesus, sharing the gospel.

September 29

Without Jesus' gospel, which is his words, you have no gospel, no church, no faith, and no salvation. You have nothing but a hell-bound religion. And that is what millions of churchgoers have because they have discarded Jesus' Word. All they have now is a fable, a nightmare and the wrath of God to come. They freely chose this fate. Are you ignoring and rejecting God's warnings? Have you read A.W. Tozer books?

September 30

Is it possible the ravening wolves are the pastors in our churches? The Bible says they are! Jeremiah 23:25-29 reveals how they operate, standing boldly giving dreamy sermons to the people. God never ordained them! Jesus said it too in Matthew 7:15. Read Acts 2:29. Isaiah 30:10.

CHAPTER 10

October 1

The easy way to heaven is to join a church, listen to pastor sermons, and don't bother to evangelize to personally share the gospel to the lost. That is the wide path that millions take. This is certainly not the narrow way, that "few" will find it. Pastor deception is blinding millions from following the true gospel and Jesus of Nazareth. Matthew 24:11.

October 2

Remember this! Apostates preach a counterfeit gospel and a counterfeit Jesus. This is their great secret and a strong and powerful magnet of power to influence people. Their preaching seems so biblically correct it will absolutely fool you if you are Biblically illiterate and brainwashed with false teachings. 2 Peter 2:1.

October 3

It is terrible deception 99.99% of churchgoers each week gather to listen to a pastor tell stories and mix in some snippets of the Word. Yet, even listening to the Word is 100% unbiblical. That is right. James 1:22 gives a dire warning that you will be deceived if you merely hear the Word of God. So even if a good Bible-teaching pastor is your pastor, you can still be deceived. How come pastors don't teach this? Do not merely listen to the Word, and so deceive yourselves. Do what it says! I John 2:18.

October 4

The only time a pastor preaches fear of God sermons is to get you to fear missing church services or if you don't have a pastor in authority over you... you will go to hell. This is wicked manipulation. Never will he preach the fear of God as God writes it in His Bible. Result is, churchgoers do not fear the Lord at all. They love the Lord with no fear and that is unbiblical. Result, they fail to respect and obey the Bible. Even Paul said you should work out your salvation with fear and trembling. 2 Cor. 11:13.

October 5

Look at your "to-do" calendar. Is there anything listed reminding you to share the gospel with the lost? How about your daily or weekly shopping list? Is there anything to remind you to purchase gospel tracts? Why not make up your list right now? Don't wait for your pastor to remind you because he won't. Don't be the one who honors God with lips, but your heart is far from him. Matthew 15:8. Do you serve your pastor?

October 6

Where are your investments? This is where your heart is. Have you invested anything into your own personal ministry that will store treasure in heaven? Colossians 3:2 commands you to do so. Have you become self-serving rather than God serving?

October 7

Matthew 5:16 commands you to let your light shine before men, that they may see your good works to Glorify your Father. Write down the good works people saw you do last week. Was there any last month? Did your pastor suggest any for you to do? What did he say? How come pastors and churchgoers do not obey the Bible? It is the mystery of iniquity in your church working to stop you from obeying God's Word.

October 8

Is your pastor busy working to develop new church programs, which supposedly provide a superior way to do the work of the Lord? If so, you are being duped! Sharing the gospel to the lost using the same methods the early church used is what worked then and still works today. You go witness to the lost. That is what God commands and wills for you to do. You don't need pastor programs that only bear bad fruit.

October 9

A church grows larger until it fills to humongous capacity is still an apostate church. Attendance or wealth has no bearing on authenticity. The Bible reveals that less is always better than more. The path is still a narrow road to heaven and few will find it. Timothy 4:1.

October 10

When you refuse to obey Jesus' commands you are rejecting and denying him despite your loyal church attendance. Then the trusted wolf, clad in wool, will snare you with a certain death grip, make merchandise of you to support his ministry to snare others into error and you will have a wonderfully strong, happy apostate church to call your very own. Matt. 7:15 Acts 20:29.

October 11

Ignoring Jesus' commands doesn't make them go away. You can forget as your pastor leads you away from Jesus with his endearing sermons, but Jesus still commands you to go save the lost, etc. Ignore God's will and directives at your own peril. Your pastor is permitting you to disobey the Lord and he falsely assures you of heaven. The Bible, Jesus your Lord, says only those who do the will of the Father are going to heaven.

October 12

You must love God above your pastor and your church. Church goers can't separate themselves from apostate pastors because the pastor has told them over and over that church attendance is crucial for salvation. Keeping God's Word by obeying Him is way more important than obeying a pastor or attending church - 1 John 2:5. The Lord never said church attendance will save you. Churchianity is not Christianity. 2 Tim. 3:5.

October 13

Do pastors lie? God says they do. He warns you of false teachers, to beware of false prophets, to be on guard for those using His name as a badge of authenticity. Many such warnings exist, yet churchgoers are blinded by Satan to see the demon standing in the pulpit preaching "another" Jesus and "another" gospel. Romans 16:17.

October 14

Apostate pastors are not anointed by God, but are anointed by the devil. They have clever speech and brilliant personalities that make them shine with great light in the pulpit and beyond. You can easily see through them though. They will never teach you how to go save the lost! Watch for that one major flaw and they can't fool you anymore. Watch the TV ministers and you will see this gaping hole in all of their heavenly captivating sermons. Most all pastors do the same today. Matthew 24:24.

October 15

Pastors that preach for revival are just playing church. They create a great craving for more religious experiences. Don't be fooled! The Bible 100% says there will be no revival in the last days. None! Zero! Things will wax worse and worse. Even Jesus said no faith would be found on the earth - Luke 18:8. The churchgoers today ignore God's commands and that is a great sign of "no faith" even in the Christian church. They are not faithful to God's Word and they don't even care to be!

October 16

Pastors think nothing of pursuing fees for preaching! God forbids it! Pastors are to feed the sheep, not fleece them. They are to give the Word freely according to Jesus command, never to sell God's Word for profit. Pastors are making money doing what the Bible said not to do. Such bold arrogance! I John 3:7.

October 17

Apostatize means they professed to believe in the Word of God, and then moved away from it. Sounds like a description of the folks who listen and obey their pastor instead of the Bible. It is easy to be an apostate. Join a church, listen to pastor sermons and never read and obey Jesus' commands. Ignore the disciples commands too while you are at it. Just tune out Jesus and turn on to the pastor. It's so easy anyone can do it.

October 18

You are told to examine yourself to make sure you are in the truth. You use the Word of God, the KJV Bible, as the "foundation" in which to build and a sound dividing of the Word to properly interpret the Word. Listening to pastor sermons amazingly uses the Word, but misapply it to create illusions to blind and mislead you into serving himself. The trickery easily fools all levels of educated people. Read apostasy books listed at JamesRussellPublishing.com

October 19

Beware of pastor's rearing robes. They are puffing themselves up to appear special and Godly. Behold the little anti-Christ! Matthew 23:5 *"But all their works they do to be seen of men: they make broad their phylacteries, and enlarge the borders of their garments."* He demands your respectful devotion and he gets it too! It is amazing the powerful influence of a costume can really be on the gullible. God never told pastors to wear priestly clothing. Does your pastor wear a costume? Beware if he does.

October 20

The truth pastors teach is the false type that makes you dependant upon them. Jesus' teachings of absolute truth will set you free from all pastors, denominations and false religions. Pastors set up their church services in such a manner so as they are seen standing in a sanctuary, a sort of perceived holy place, so that to get to God you must go through him. All eyes are upon him. Pastor become the mediator. 1 Timothy 2:5.

October 21

Pastors proclaim you are backsliding if you do not attend church. The Bible never teaches you must attend church! Today's church is not a fellowshipping of the saints. It is a pastor's building owned by the pastor or denomination and is controlled by rigid programs and the people truly do not fellowship. Church buildings never existed in the Early Church, nor is their mention of even desiring one to be built... not one! The people were the church and they gathered in homes in small groups. The church building is unbiblical and is not a true church. It is a counterfeit fooling millions of people. Galatians 1:6.

October 22

Pastors want you to believe you are faithful saved Christians, but you are just churchgoers who think you are saved! Jesus said you must be born-again. Most all churchgoers are not! You can tell because they have no mercy to save the lost and they choose to disobey Jesus' commands each and every day. Jesus has friends and He has enemies. *"Ye are my friends, if you do whatsoever I command you."* Keep obeying your pastor

MOM! HE'S BACK!
IT'S THAT PASTOR AGAIN!

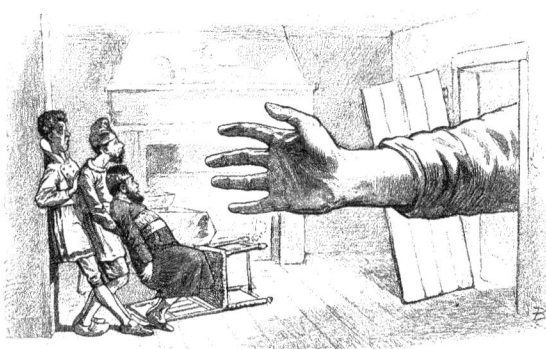

HE WON'T LET GO!

There is a pastor waiting to rule you and teach you mighty things you did not know and all you have to do is let him into your life and serve him. It's that easy! But the moment you try to start your own ministry to save the lost his mighty hand of horror will be revealed. He may even cast you out of his church and condemn you to hell.

Every denomination, including the Protestants and the little independent church on the corner is operating in deceit to trick you into becoming a Christian, but its a form a godliness that denies the power of God. The power is truly the pastors' power and if you join that church you will serve him believing you are serving God. That is the great falling away right before your very eyes, but few see it and escape!

THE LION WILL GET YOU!

Have you noticed that pastors preach often that if a man stops going to church he will backslide and the devil will get him? But what he is preaching to you is a outright lie and it is not Biblical whatsoever. Jesus and his disciples never preached or taught these things.

Of all the warnings given in the Bible there is <u>not one instance</u> of warning telling the believer to go to church or go to hell. Not one warning that if you do not go to church you are backsliding. Not one warning that if you skip church attendance the wolves and lions will get you. Not one instance. If God wanted you to go to church each week he would have told you to do so. He told you to rest each Sabbath day, not go to church! Read your Bible!

Your pastor desperately wants you to go to church to support him financially, but his heart is very far away from actually teaching you how to go save the lost, which is your Christian duty, and it is his job to teach you how as a church leader! But your pastor has a different agenda. He wants to control you and get you to obey him, not Jesus!

Impossible you say! Not my pastor! But the truth is, every pastor is misleading his people and dragging them away from actually "obeying" the gospel while he teaches you to become "hearers" of the gospel, not <u>doers</u>!

and you will be Jesus' enemy. You can't serve both.

October 23

So you are afraid to go proclaim the gospel to the Lord? Then prepare for hell fire. The Bible deems you equal to an unbeliever, a liar, the abominable, murderer, whoremongers, homosexuals, prostitutes, sorcerers and idolaters. All are going to hell, including the "fearful" who refuse to risk persecution for obeying the Lord. Your pastor cultivates a great crop of fear to keep you in his garden of bondage. You worship God in vain when you disobey Him. John 7:24.

October 24

Pastors are master liars. They omit certain scriptures and only include those that fit their doctrine. The result is a sermon laced with lies perceived to be Biblical truth! He bears a false witness breaking the 9th Commandment and he is an intentional liar of the worse kind. He conspires to deceive with his false teachings. Yes, the trusted pastor is the true enemy of the gospel. Beware of pastor sermons, especially so if he sells them! Luke 12:57.

October 25

Beware of pastors using the Bible to compel you to attend and support their church! It's an old trick, but it works like charm - Hebrews 10:25 and 1 Cor. 16:1-2. Always remember these verses can never apply to cults, false and apostate churches. Can you understand why? You can't be supporting ungodly endeavors when God tells you to get out from among them. Stop being fooled! Read and obey your Bible, not your pastor. Matthew 7:15-16. Does your pastor command fear of himself? Do people fear challenging his decisions? Does he rule with an iron fist and act as the ultimate authority?

October 26

Do you know your pastor heavily focuses his "church services" on praise and worship, but he ignores the important Christian duties and responsibilities? Like a loose cannon, he routinely disobeys the Lord with impunity! Jesus never commanded you to conduct or attend worship services. It's true. He never did! But He repeatedly told you numerous times to obey His commands! You are following, serving and obeying your pastor and denying Jesus. 2 Timothy 2:19.

October 27

Pastor worship is the core of false Christianity. All eyes and ears are upon him and great affection is showered upon him. He is elevated to a holy-like presence. People even stand clear a path for him to walk, as if God were passing by. Open your eyes and see! God never shares his glory with any man! It's time to kick out the pedestal on pastors playing church. In fact, they should be excommunicated, but they usually "own" the church. Instead, they will throw you out!

October 28

Gambling churchgoers are not in a casino, but in your church! They bet that their pastor is right, but he could be wrong too. That's a 50% chance of being deceived and ending up in hell! Las Vegas has way better odds than this! If you follow, serve, support and obey a pastor you are in great danger! A sure bet is to follow, serve, support, and obey Jesus of Nazareth. That's like hitting the jackpot 100%. Place your bets ladies and gentlemen! You can choose Jesus or your pastor, as you can't serve both.

October 29

When a pastor's main focus is to preach sermons and nobody gets on fire to save the lost or preach the gospel you need to come out of that church. 2 Cor. 6:17. Turn away: 2 Tim. 3:5. Withdraw yourself; 2 Thess. 3:6. Have not fellowship with them; Eph. 5:11. The fruit is the sermon and it malnourishes the soul making you hungry for God's Word, but with a strangeness of not wanting to obey the Word of God.

October 30

God promised the church would be filled with false prophets. Pastors are those prophets. 1 John 4:1. They are the church leaders. The ones who are doing the teaching. God means what He says.

October 31

Not all pastors are apostate. Just 999.999 are. Yes, .001 exist. They may even own a church building and collect tithe money, but if they contend for the faith, teach all of the Word of God and prepare you to go forth to bear much good fruit and do good deeds and are doers of the Word as Jesus said his followers would do, then you are lucky. Odds are, you are unlucky. I bet on it.

If you truly want to see the truth of apostasy in your church, ask your pastor to preach on the following subjects. He won't do it! Later I will tell you why. Be forewarned. Your church is not the church of Jesus Christ! Ask your pastor to;

1. Expose and renounce other religious beliefs that are apostate and unbiblical. Name the names of these deceiving pastors and religions! Warn the flock of this danger and tell us how to protect ourselves.

2. Declare that your church is controlled by Jesus Christ and him alone as the head and that there is no other authority controlling your church; not the government or secular laws.

3. Preach that your church will preach against homosexuals being members of your church.

4. Preach "politically incorrect" sermons condemning any and all apostasies infiltrating true Christianity. The flock must be fed the entire true gospel of God's word without restriction or interference by the government and other non-church unbelievers.

5. Preach on every subject mentioned in the Bible that God hates and disapproves. Idolaters, homosexuals, prostitutes, false religions, false shepherds, lying church denominations, thieves, murderers, etc.

6. Tell us who to vote for in politics that will benefit society, the church or Christians. Endorse the candidate of choice and this will help to oppose the anti-Christian candidate. Publish some or all of this advice in our (your) church newsletter.

7. Expose the abortion clinics in town. Tell us who these doctors are and let us protest them with demonstrations to stop the murder of innocent babies.

8. Voice your concern of certain politicians enacting legislation that will harm Christians. The flock must be warned of pending danger!

9. Expose the false teachers in other churches, so we won't be lured by them into their trap. Protect the flock like the apostles did!

10. Preach the truth. Tell us that anti-Christ (unchurched people) is not in our church controlling it. Tell us we do not have these people (the government) telling our pastor, bishop, elders or deacons what they can or can not preach in the pulpit. Tell us it is not so!

11. Preach that our church serves and obeys only Jesus Christ and if the government says we can't preach about certain subjects, we will obey Jesus, not the government. Preach what the Bible says is wrong regardless, just as the apostles did. They obeyed and served one Master, not two.

12. Tell us if the state government owns our church via incorporation laws and what rules we must follow or else we can lose our church due to government confiscation and even imprison us! We must know if Jesus is the true, sole head of our church or are we really serving two masters! Tell us how we can be unincorporated to regain our freedom!

13. Preach to us the truth that our pastor is really turning over our names to the government, reporting our donations of time and money and other private church matters. Tell us it is not so you are reporting on us and prove it.

14. Tell us it is not true that our pastor is a "hireling" of the state, that he is an "officer" of the state, doing state business! He is serving two masters.

15. Tell us if our (your) church is a legal incorporation whereas our church must remain silent on subjects the state deems is politically incorrect? Or are we a free church subject to complete freedom of speech, like our constitution permits. If we are not free, how can we get free? Tell us!

16. Tell us is it true our pastor, our bishop, our elders, our deacons are "trustees" subject to state incorporation laws that can prevent them from preaching Biblical truths and that they sit at the pleasure of the state and can be removed by the state for preaching God's Word the state finds to be offensive. Tell us!

17. Tell us it is not true that our (your) church property is not held in trust for God, but is held in trust for the state. If so, tell us how to be free of these shackles.

18. Please preach the truth that if the state condones homosexuals we must now let them be members of our church. Even let them hold church positions of authority? Even if the Bible condemns it?

19. Tell us, is it true you, our pastor "must" preach in your pulpit that we church members "must" pay our taxes? Why are you conducting sermons that are not church business? You do this each April! Did the state "order" you to do this? Be truthful to us!

20. Tell us you are not submitting the names if all church members,

even maintenance workers to the government? Why are you conducting this non-church business?

21. Publicly oppose the licensing of cult churches being planned in our city!

22. Engage in political activity to renounce and oppose pornography in our city, state or country. Stand in the gap! Warn the people!

23. Form a committee to support legislation opposing lotteries and gambling and pornography.

24. Oppose the school system! They are teaching our children filth and unbiblical practices.

25. Publicly stand up for God and let your light shine before men! Go outside the walls of the church and preach that the church is to obey God rather than man's government, just like the apostles said and did. Let us go with you!

26. Tell us you are patriotic and not a traitor and that you will support the U.S. or State constitutions and declare to us it is the supreme law of the land, or have you signed away this right too? We need to know which master you are really serving!

Many churches are unincorporated from state rulership, because a tax exempt pastor/church can't do any of the above. Really! A church need not be incorporated. It is a choice! It's usually done by greedy pastors and denominations to obtain tax-free status. This has always been a handshake with the world! Serving two masters! Any entity that restricts preaching the full Bible; the good, the bad and the ugly is antichrist! Most all churches are incorporated and have sold their soul to Satan's control. That's why your pastor "omits" certain sermons and why you are never taught all truth! The church needs a total overhaul.

A business sponsors a gay pride parade in your town. Your pastor can't speak out, lobby or oppose the wickedness. He must remain silent.

**THE SIN OF WITCHCRAFT
IT IS IN <u>YOUR</u> CHURCH!**

November 1

Who gave Biblical authority for pastors to conduct funeral services? Did a pastor perform a service when Jesus or the apostles died? Not according to the Bible. This is another example of pastors meddling where they do not belong! There is no Biblical example or authority given to them to do most everything they do. It has gotten way out of line. Jesus said, *"Let the dead bury the dead..."*

November 2

The foundation of the modern visible organized church is totally 100% corrupt and satanic. It has veered way out of line from the New Testament church and gospel teachings. It is so flawed it must be dismantled and rebuilt. More likely, you will need to separate and come out of her, the established church - Rev 18:1-5. Don't wait until the pastor or trustee errs and the state swoops in arresting church member. It's happening! Get out of these physical-building apostate churches as fast as you can! Get back to the Bible. Meet in your homes! 1 Peter 4:17.

November 3

Substitution – remember that word. It is the great secret key how apostasy operates. How? Simply bend the truth just a little bit by substituting Jesus with another Jesus. Replace the easy yoke of the gospel with another gospel, substituting the real for the counterfeit. Substitute God's Word with the pastor's words (sermons). Replace God's commands with another requirement that you need not obey. Omit God's agenda with rules created by men and their tradition. Worship replaces obedience to God's desires and supersedes saving the lost, etc. Substitution – Never forget this is how apostates succeed, like magic. 2. Cor. 11:3-13.

November 4

Women pastors and women speaking in the formal fellowship are still prohibited. We may not like it, but the Bible is clear on this matter. 1 Tim. 2:12, 1 Cor. 14:34-3, (Acts 17:9 the four virgins were not teaching anyone, God spoke through them). This is another disobedience churches routinely perform. We can not disobey God's Word and then go on praising and praying to God. That is playing church. If Paul and Timothy said

CHAPTER 11
The New Gospel

not to do it, and you dismiss their word, then never quote Paul or Timothy ever again in your church! And that includes Jesus. If your church disobeys Jesus' commands you have no church! You worship in vain. Follow God's rules or get out of Christianity. You are wasting your time. Rev. 2:1-5.

November 5

Pastors by the tens of thousands preach to millions upon millions of churchgoers that they are saved. But what if Jesus is right? He said that few would be saved! Few! Few! Few! Not multi-millions! Who is the liar? I would say the pastors are lying, wouldn't you? Jesus said many are called but "few" are chosen. Now what if rapture does take place and God only takes a few? Say a few thousand? Then millions will be left behind!

November 6

If you end up in hell you will have an excuse. Jesus said many will be there grinding their teeth in outer darkness, forever. You may be lonely for all eternity with nobody to see or talk to, but you will have an excuse! You were deceived by your pastor! Your second excuse is you did not take the Bible seriously and you disregarded Jesus' warning, *"Do not be deceived."* You even chose to ignore these warnings in these pages. Yes, you certainly do have an excuse to be in hell. It is not too late right now to come back to your Father. Jesus is calling you, *"I am the good shepherd!"* 2 Cor. 13:5.

November 7

Pastors know that they should be teaching you how to go save the lost, but they compromise themselves, disobey the Lord and preach other things. The #1 priority of Christians is to go save the lost, the Great Commission, and that is precisely what is not being done! In fact, it is ignored! This is what Satan desires; praise the Lord but disobey Him. This creates an insulting and shameful injury to the Lord, and a church full of disobedient hypocrites and sons who are actually bastards!

November 8

Is the Synagogue of Satan the modern day church? Well, this is nothing new at all. The term is used in the New Testament, so it should be of no surprise to realize the same old tricks are being employed today. Are you being blinded by Satan and his church to not see the Great Apostasy?

November 9

Be extremely careful when a pastor demands to be your spiritual authority or to be your shepherd! He will even use fear of the devil getting you if you have no shepherd (him). He is a liar. Jesus is the Good Shepherd! Without Jesus, the devil *will* get you. You can not and must not trust the apostate churches and their spiritual leaders. It is a satanic trap to do so! Do you want to submit to the enemy of God; the apostate pastor? You may already be doing so. It is better to be churchless and serve the Good Lord than to be churched into the lion's teeth! 2 John 7,10-11.

November 10

Is your pastor living in a mansion or an expensive home? Does he have expensive cars and an upscale lifestyle? Is his lifestyle even better than most all of his congregation? This is your greatest warning that you have a money-grabbing, tithe-stealing pastor making merchandise of you. Pastors earning wealth selling the gospel is unbiblical. The Bible even warns you about these false teachers. Have you read the Biblical warnings?

November 11

The tithe lies. There is no command in the New Testament Bible to give tithes to a pastor or to his church. It's true! A collection can be made to "share" with other church members. It is 100% unbiblical for tithe money to be taken by pastors to enrich him or to build church buildings. Wake up! You are being fleeced and your tithe will bear no fruit in God's eyes. The Bible reveals the truth and you need to read it, especially how the Early Church is ordained to function. Your pastor is violating the rules more than you know! Invest your tithe to purchase gospel tracts to reach the lost. Malachi 3:10 is Old Testament. Go read it for yourself.

November 12

Begging pastors! The Lord never commands pastors, ministers or any other Christian to plead, coerce or beg Christians for money to support their ministry. It is an outright abomination for pastors to create sympathetic, emotional, heartfelt sermons to entice Christians to give them money. The Lord pays the bills, not schemes and scams. Beware of the apostate churches operating unlike the Early Church. They funnel money away from the flock to spend it on themselves.

November 13

Don't be fooled! Perhaps as small as 2% of tithe money goes to the "cause" while the rest of the money is put into a special bank account. A pastor can legally keep every penny you give to him for it is deemed a gift. That position of power was never granted by the Bible. Apostle Paul worked as a tent maker and still became the greatest church builder. He did not abuse believers by begging for their tithe or other monies and not one physical church was ever built nor was one desired. The church building itself is an improper foundation and a clear violation of Biblical intent and purpose. Open your eyes!

November 14

To see right through a deceiving pastor's sermon just ask yourself as you listen, *"Is anyone here going to be motivated to go share the gospel to the lost?"* Will you be excited and actually go proclaim the gospel? That's how you can decipher these storytelling pastors. They are not interested in saving the lost! They are not interested in teaching anyone how to save the lost. They are not even interested in your own welfare and standing with God. Always remember to ask, *"Is this sermon going to help me save the lost for Jesus?"* If not, the pastor is throwing you a bag of wind. Acts 17:11.

November 15

Where are the warnings not to slide into apostasy? Sermon after sermon after sermon and still no warnings by pastors! Why? Because they make you think it is not required. They also think God does not mind them not protecting the flock. Hebrews 6:4-6. They have a reservation prepared in the lake of fire. A special place for false teachers.

THE GOLDEN DREAM

Pastors are trouble for you and obstructions to God's work. You see, God wants the lost to be saved and he wants his people to go share the gospel with the lost every day. But your pastor has a different idea. He wants a nice big fancy church with a day school, Sunday school, and he wants to earn a huge salary by taking God's tithe money that you give to him and steal it for his own dream.

That's the conflict of interest pastors have. They want a big church and big money and they develop sermons to get you to give them your money. But they all do one thing in common. They won't teach you how to go save the lost!

When (or if) you ever go passing out gospel tracts you will find yourself all alone and your pastor will not buy those gospel tracts for you unless you put his church name on them to draw more people into his sticky web! He will never stop begging for money and that too is unbiblical. God does not authorize begging of money by pastors!

MONEY IS OUR GOSPEL!

Go ahead and read your Bible one more time and look to see where Jesus said for pastors to be going about begging for money. You won't find it. But you will find plenty of warnings of the "hireling" who does not care about the sheep and you will read about false prophets and untrustworthy shepherds who desire to deceive you and make merchandise of you. The Bible warns you of it!

But for some reason, people just think they can disobey Jesus and ignore his commands and warnings and get away with it. Well, the bad news is... you will get deceived!

Jesus warned you and he sends people into your life to warn you of danger, but if you keep on listening, trusting and believing your pastor and his lies you will discover the error in your ways all too late. And don't think you are going to heaven for disobeying your Lord, he warned you about hell too, didn't he? He certainly did, but your pastor dismisses all Jesus' warnings of hell and makes you believe the "once saved, always saved" lie. As if Christian disobedient cheats, liars, thieves, rapists, murderers, homosexuals, prostitutes, etc., are going to heaven? Who are you kidding?

November 16

Once you have asked the Lord to remove the blindness Satan has put on you, apostasy in the churches will clearly be seen. You will even wonder how you missed all the dozens of warnings in the Bible! Warnings upon warnings are being ignored by churchgoers, and pastors are responsible for evading God's warnings. Saint Paul, John, Jude, Jesus all gave multiple warnings not to veer from the truth. All you need do is read the Bible to see it. The broad way is still the wrong way!

November 17

Read Acts 20:29-30. It will tell you that the apostasy will come from within the church. Savage wolves and teachers will devour the flock. The entire visible church has been infiltrated and destroyed. None are Biblical and all have gone astray. And that is the description given to us by the Bible in the time of the last days. Let us see what we can get from the Lord and see that we will not repay Him for we will not give Him what He wants in return. This is the deep core message in the church today. A tiny remnent remains. Tiny means very small, nil, hardly seen. Not all of the many people in all the churches we see today.

November 18

Who is the lawless one? Who is the antichrist? It is the false shepherds and their deceived flocks. They think nothing of disobeying the Bible. Satan has got them to believe that apostate teachings are the truth! Scary, isn't it. They are the religious faith criminals and outlaws professing loyalty to Christ in word, but not in deed. Rebellious hypocrites.

November 19

Every retired Christian, including those hireling retired pastors, should be out reaching the lost every day, no exceptions! They have the time and most also have the money to do so, but they won't go. Their true spirit is of their father the devil, just like the Lord said. Beware of these false churchgoing elders who care not to share the gospel to the lost. They are false elders and poor examples. Do not obey or follow their example.

November 20

Don't be fooled by pastors getting you to perform charitable works in the community like cleaning sidewalks, painting and fixing homes, etc. This misguided service is not Biblical. You need to stop this nonsense and go to work doing what Jesus commanded; proclaim the gospel. Jesus never told anyone to perform community service work. Do not replace individual salvation for helping one's neighbors for it is not the function of the the true beliver. Remember the word "substitution" ?

November 21

Matt. 7:15 and 24:11-24 warns you will not recognize the wolf in your church, until it is too late. He will be in a position of authority and totally disguised. He will absolutely fool you! Satan fooled a third of the angels in heaven taking them down with a lie and Adam and Eve. Your pastor will be the instrument Satan will use to take you down. Paul warned he will devour the entire flock and spare none! Do not follow pastors. Read your Bible so you can escape. Do not touch the unclean thing.

November 22

Amazingly, pastors are telling all attending their church, *"You are saved! You are saved!"* Satan told Eve, *"Ye shall not surely die."* Gen. 3:4-5. His ministers are pulling the wool over their eyes with the same old lie! You won't go to hell. You can't backslide. Jesus never taught such nonsense. You may be face to face with the Devil in your church. His charisma will be pleasent to behold.

November 23

Any that thrust people away from God with false teachings should be stoned - Deut. 13:1-2,5,10. This means most all pastors qualify because they do not teach or preach all of what Jesus and apostles taught and said and that creates a false Jesus and a false gospel. Those who follow and believe these lying pastors despise the Lord of the Bible. Rebelious idolators! Jesus said in the last days there will be a great falling away from the faith. How come your pastor fails to mention this falling away? As if it is not even happening!

November 24

What is sad is pastors have so much Biblical knowledge, yet they will not do any open air street preaching to reach the lost. That's what Jesus and his disciples did! Today pastors "hide" in their church and care not to reach the lost. Think about that! They won't even teach church members how to do it. There is a great famine in the land. God's Word is hidden from the people. This is as unchristian as it gets, but this is the pastor's desire. He will not change!

November 25

You don't have to be an apostate. Apostasy is a choice! At first, some trusted fast-talking con artist pastor fools you. It happens to the best Christians, even the very elect. Then, the Lord in His mercy shows you the truth in His Word in His Bible about deceivers. It is at this point you choose the Lord or your pastor, the Lord or your faith, the Lord or your beliefs, the Lord or your denomination. If you try to follow both the Lord and anything else, you'll despise the Lord. Usually, Christians reject God's messengers and reject God's Word, like the Jews did. Apostasy is your choice. The warnings are all in the Bible.

November 26

Few have the courage to stand for truth. Most churchgoers are too busy sitting in the pew or kneeling before their pastor to be bothered to contend for the faith one delivered to the saints. No wonder the Bible says the fearful shall not enter heaven. These cowards will not obey the commands of Jesus. They won't save the lost and they do not "seek" the lost. But they do have the courage to break the laws. They ignore God's laws and even man's laws. They won't save the lost for Christ and they say to excuse themselves, *"It is not my calling."* They love to speed in their cars, violating speed limits with great impunity and refuse to use their turn signals making life hard and dangerous to other drivers. This spirit of lawlessness spills over from church life to normal life. Just follow them to or from church and you will witness this truth.

November 27

You watch that reckless renegade pastor on television and you listen carefully to his blasphemies blessing and promising everlasting life to the wicked that has deceased. That's right, a funeral for an ungodly, unsaved rich or famous person. They quote the Lord's promises and His Psalms reserved for His saints and this deceiving pastor gives those promises to those who serve demons in life, but now are dead. Notice also the expensive business suite or religious "costume" that pastor may wear to glorify himself. Pastors have no place to be performing Christian services to the wicked or make false promises to the deceased. Is there no decency? Not with funeral pastors! Jesus said it plain and clear to let the dead bury their dead. Get away from the apostate pastors and expose them.

November 28

Do you want to know a frightening truth? If you are not on fire witnessing to the lost, you have lost your power for service. The Lord has rejected you due to sin in your life. That sin can be your choice to follow and obey your pastor disregarding the commands of the Lord. See 1 Cor.9:29, Zech. 4:6 and Lk. 1:31-35. Jesus said to go share the gospel. You had better stop disobeying him. Also read 2 Tim. 3:5 and turn away from all who disobey the Lord and have a form of religion even those who claim to be Christians. A true Christian obeys the Lord.

November 29

Read your Bible to see that Satan uses the "leaders" to lead the way against God. Those leaders today are the pastors in your church and they lead millions into the great apostasy. The sheep are following the wrong shepherd! When you reject and ignore Jesus' commands you are rejecting him - John 12:48. You keep your pastor's commands, but ignore Jesus; *"If you love Me, keep my commandments."* - John 14:15. Attending worship services in a church building once each week is unbiblical. None of the apostles did this nor commanded it.

November 30

Gambling churchgoers are not in a casino, but in your church! They bet that their pastor is right, but he could be wrong too. That's a 50% chance of being deceived and ending up in hell! Las Vegas has way better odds than this! If you follow, serve, support and obey a pastor you are in

CHAPTER 12

SOMETHING AIN'T RIGHT

You ain't kidding something ain't right. Jesus warned us there would be wolves's in sheep clothing passing themselves off as being devout religious leaders and we now know <u>they are the pastors</u>! False teachers are always nice people!

Jesus also said there would be "many" not a few, but "<u>MANY</u>" deceivers among us. It is time you open your eyes and see what Jesus warned us about. Jesus also said that they would deceive many, not a few, but "<u>MANY</u>" so pay attention because it can happen to <u>YOU and it likely is already and you don't know it</u>!

great danger! A sure bet is to follow, serve, support, and obey Jesus.

THERE IS SO MUCH YOU CAN DO

Most churchgoers are not performing good works. Sure, many work at soup kitchens and homeless missions to feed and clothe the poor, but Jesus also has one more big job that takes priority; to go share the gospel with the lost.

I have seen many churches perform good works for the community, but they are "silent" and will <u>not</u> share the gospel when doing these good works. You miss the mark!

God wants the lost to be saved! Do both. Do the charitable work, but also never neglect sharing the gospel. Why ignore the latter?

Pastors will get you to clean and paint homes, yards and city parks all to perform charity good-will community work, but where are the thousands of gospel tracts to be handed out? Are they just sitting on some table going nowhere? If so, hand them out to the people.

I have seen Christians operating display booths at many public functions and they just sit behind the table with a stack of literature. It is like standing by a river watching the fish swim by. They won't bother to stick a fishing line into the water to catch a fish. Sadly, they think they are doing a good work, a good deed for the Lord. They are <u>not obeying</u> the Lord at all. Did Jesus operate a booth? Did the apostles? They did not sit back and wait for people to come to them. They went fishing for the people. Do likewise. Get out from behind the table and share the gospel.

Churchgoers think that increasing church membership is effective evangelization. What if you recruited 1,000 people to join your church only to find out later the church is apostate? All of your work is now worthless and you sent 1,000 people and countless more to hell. That is the *danger* of working for a pastor to recruit new church members. It is <u>not</u> Christian. Read your Bible. Nobody went out recruiting. They went out and preached the Word of God, the gospel and the Lord made the increase and nobody went to church like they do today. They met in homes.

December 1

King Jeroboam made Israel to sin by creating a new way to worship 1 Kings 12:25-33. Jacob did too. God revealed where to assemble in the New Testament, and it was not in Temples or church buildings! It was to be in homes! Your pastor refuses to preach this truth! Your pastor is wrong and all who enter these unbiblical places of worship. They are built on sand. Beware of ministries planting church (buildings). Paul planted churches with no buildings to show for it. Physical churches defy the revealed will of God. Come out of them!

December 2

Imagine a police officer who runs away from the thief and letting the robber escape or a fireman who lets a house burn and ignores the victim's pleas for help, or a fisherman who looks at the catch, but will not cast his net. Imagine a lawyer refused to do his job to defend you, or the surgeon not wearing protective gloves or face mask. All are renegades! So it is with the pastor's lazy flock. They will not go share the gospel to the lost. The pastor does not mind this at all as long as the money keeps on rolling in. This pastor is wrongly dividing the Word of truth! The fruit is bitter. The lost are not hearing the gospel. A kingdom of cowards!

December 3

The modern pastor is not as modern as you believe. They cause division and offences contrary to Biblical teachings by mixing up sermons with psychology feel-good-ism into an intoxicating brew of deceit to fool the simple. And they do it using the Bible in hand as a shield to conceal their false interpretations of God's Word. It's going on inside your very own church! And your Bible commands you to depart from him. Rom. 16:17-18.

December 4

Do you know you will not escape God's full wrath if you fail to warn the wicked from his wicked ways? It's true. Ezekiel 3:18 promises you will be held fully accountable and blamed for it, too. Your pastor, denomination, church membership and beliefs will not save you when the Lord punishes you. Witnessing is deadly serious business! Pastors don't care to teach, preach or warn of these Words from God. Have you no fear of the Lord? Have you no wisdom? God's Word is praised, but not obeyed.

December 5

So, you are afraid to go share the gospel to the lost? Blame yourself. The Bible does not tell you to blindly obey your pastor waiting for him to tell you to perform Jesus' commands. John 3:20 reveals the sin of cowardness! But you now have your second chance. Get your gospel tracts and get going. If you refuse, go read Matt. 13:15 and you can forget about God hearing your pleas for help in your time of healing! What if Martin Luther feared the Bishop, Cardinal or Pope there would be no Protestants!

December 6

This book will destroy your cheap faith! The Bible says you don't need a pastor to get to heaven! 1 Tim. 2:5. If you do not obey (by doing) Jesus' commands you are a liar and all liars go into the lake of fire 1 John 2:4. Satan has ministers teaching you. 2 Cor 11:15. Yes, you! You think antichrist means those who act evil, but anyone who replaces Jesus Christ or his gospel is antichrist and that's what pastors do today. Remember that word, substitution!

December 7

Why do pastors retain disobedient brethren in their church when they are to be removed? 2 Thes. 3:6, 14,15.

December 8

Are you aware Jesus had so little to say about the church, its functions, programs, methodology? So, where are the pastor's marching orders coming from? Who is giving them the permission and authority to do and preach and teach what they do? Show me where the Bible tells pastors to build church buildings and conduct worship services and command them to take God's tithe money? You should be asking yourself such questions.

December 9

The Jews said, *"We will not have this man reign over us."* - Lk. 19:14.

They also would not do the things Jesus says - Lk. 6:46. That is what pastor-directed churches are teaching the flock today. Churchgoing Christians don't have to obey Jesus anymore and it is okay to ignore Jesus' sayings, but Jesus calls those who do this, fools - Matt. 7:26. Pastors are ignoring and rejecting the teachings of Jesus and pushing their sermons instead, a false gospel. Jesus is not welcome in church because he says hard and harsh things. Pastors cover up these Words of Jesus diligently by willful design. A Christianity without Christ!

December 10

What are you doing to?
1. Reach homosexuals.
1. Reach Mormons.
2. Reach Roman Catholics.
3. Reach Jehovah Witnesses.
4. Reach the homeless.
5. Reach the poor.
6. Reach our troubled youth.
7. Reach the elderly.
8. Reach prostitutes.
9. Reach drug users.
10. Reach the lost for Christ.

Be merciful. Who are you reaching out to share the gift of eternal life? Why is your pastor not teaching you how? If church is just to listen to a pastor's sermons, then you will end up a do-nothing Christian that will be cut off the vine. Jesus promises you it will be so. Go share the gospel. That is your job! If not, then don't be a Christian. Stop playing games. Mercy covers a multitude of sins. Have you no mercy upon the lost?

December 11

The pulpits are occupied by unqualified ministers who are teaching everything but Biblical commands. They may mention you must obey, but they don't tell you "what to do to comply" with the Lord's commands. They talk up a storm and in the end nobody can say they see the light. *"Why call ye Me Lord, Lord, and do not the things which I say?"* Lk. 6:46. Your pastor did not die for your sins, yet you revere his word over the Lord's Word. You obey your pastor. Awake from your slumber! Jesus said you must forsake all (Lk. 14:33) but you will not give up your church or your pastor to follow Jesus. The apostles had to give up their Jewish church and their Jewish pastors. So will you. You are on a wide and easy way leading you to hell. Matt. 7:14. The Lord means what He says. Church-folks have found the easy way with pastors assuring them they don't have to obey the Lord or witness to the lost. Just believe the pastor and you are saved. It's believing fables and lies.

December 12

Above the apostate pastor's head is a banner with a word inscribed, *"Ichabod"* that the blind cannot, and those who have worldly eyes, will not see. It means, *"The glory has departed."* - 1 Sam. 4:2. The pastor sets up an emotion-driven environment inside his church building designed by him to simulate the presence of God. A pastor manufactured glory! This is a glory not of God. Elders take heed of Acts 20:27-31. The pastors have gone astray!

December 13

What if everyone in your church were not Christians? If we are in the last age then we are deep into the Great Apostasy just as the Bible said will exist. This means most to all churchgoers are not Christians. This is not a far fetch idea. Just look at all the false religions and it becomes a sobering reality. If these writings can't reach you, you need to ask the Lord to open your eyes and ears before it is too late! God has already given up on many, just as the Bible said would happen.

December 14

Apostasy is a choice. Disobeying the Lord is a choice. You stray away when you no longer can hear the voice (Word) of the Good Shepherd. You can choose not to see apostasy. You can choose not to hear Jesus' warnings and his call to obey and follow him. You can choose not to search the scriptures for truth. You can choose to let your pastor's sermons drown out the beckoning of your Lord warning you to flee from the wolf in sheep's clothing. You can choose to believe a lie. You can choose to let the lost burn in hell, but the Lord will hold you accountable and that fate in Hell you chose too!

December 15

Pastors say you won't be at the Great White Throne Judgment. Don't be so sure! If you are not born again and *doing* the will of the Father, then your name is not in His Book of Life. Most churchgoers will be screaming for mercy when they discover they were deceived by lying pastors/wolves. Jesus warned you and you willfully ignored his dire warning. The lake of fire awaits all who chose to be deceived. They chose to rebel. They followed *another* voice, *another* shepherd, *another* Jesus. They followed a pastor! Jesus said, *"Follow Me!"*

December 16

The Lord wants you to have your own personal ministry / mission. He knew pastors would create cunning false and misleading ministries to steal tithe money. There are ministries that do go into the community seeking out the lost, but beware. There is a pastor lurking nearby "umbilically begging" for money to finance his ministry/mission program. He is living in an expensive home, owns dream cars and is filthy rich in worldly investments. The lost are saved to become slave to the pastor! The Lord wants you to go bear much good fruit. Supporting a begging pastor with your time and money gives you no account of value with the Lord. It's all in vain. Get smart. Obey the Lord. Your ministry is to serve the Lord to seek those who are lost, just like Jesus did and commanded you to do. Amen! Be careful not to send new converts to an apostate church! All of your evangelism work will be wasted. Share the gospel and save the lost, but *don't* send them to a church building.

December 17

Extend yourself. You can reach the lost thousands of miles away by simply using a phone book, gospel tract, envelope and postage stamp. You have never done this because your pastor never told you to. You have "no excuse" to keep using excuses. It's time you get to work reaching out to save the lost. You can also send "Biblically correct" tracts to send to cults and other false religions. No more excuses! Invest your tithe money to share God's Word to those who need it. You owe the Lord at least to do this for Him! Do not give up. Work and endure to the end.

CAN THEY ALL BE WRONG?

Many church people foolishly believe that the majority of all the people can't be wrong. That all the churches can't be wrong. Yet they ignore their own Bible.

All the people were wrong when God destroyed the world by flood. Only Noah and his family were right. All were wrong in Sodom and Gomorrah, but Lot and his family. All were wrong when they crucified Jesus.

The Bible says in the last days there will be few with true faith and there will be a great falling away. That falling away is right here, right now, before your very eyes with false churches everywhere teaching unbiblical things, as if they were Biblical, with false pastors in every one of those churches deceiving and being deceived.

Only a few will be saved! That's what the Bible teaches, but pastors say many will be saved. All the many churchgoers! Isn't it amazing that all the churchgoers are saved? Yet we all know most churchgoers are not even saved! And many are cult members in horrible religions, but they are saved according to the pastors they serve.

To EUROPE

the Orient, Alaska, South America, "Around the World" and other Cruises. Travel in U.S. & Canada

"The Voyage of Your Dreams"

WE HAVE NO TIME

Lord, we are too busy to bother to save the lost for you. Anyway, our pastor told us by supporting his church we are doing God's will. We don't have to do anything except go to church each Sunday and get on with our own lives. Ask somebody else, not me! I'm too busy.

December 18

    Question everything! Never assume just because every church is doing it, it's okay. Not when most all churches are apostate! Also, listening to pastor sermons is a waste of time. What good is it to listen to them teach you how to do nothing to save the lost? Or learn how to ignore the Lord's commands? They talk about it, but they never teach you how to obey the Lord and save the lost. Don't be taken in by these dishonest pastors. The real mission field is where you walk! Not with some church mission business that only reproduces more useless apostate clones of itself.

December 19

    Have you noticed when preaching sermons the pastor stands among the flowers? This is all by design to appease your eye seeing your pastor in a lovely setting to fool you into believing he is holy, precious and highly esteemed. Beware of these gimmicks. The Bible warns the church leaders will lead you astray - Isaiah 9:16. They will come from within the church to deceive. Sounds like a pastor to me. What do you think? It will be a minister of righteousness. That says it all.

December 20

    You are the answer to someone's prayer. Somewhere a parent is desperately praying to God to save a wayward loved one. It could be a career criminal, prostitute, drug addict, or whatever. But the eyes of the Lord search and can find none in the churches capable or willing to go. As a result, the prayer is never answered and bitterness, misery and hell is the fruit. This is why you should be going into all areas leaving gospel tracts. It's one way to reach the lost and the Lord can now send you into places where prayers can be answered. You can be part of the solution preventing future crime, maybe even save the very person who would have killed you! Think about that. But will you serve the Lord?

December 21

    What if a pastor employs devices to excite emotional states like holy-like music and soothing moments of devout prayer then tells all the Holy Spirit is present in his church and that everybody is saved, but a "different" spirit exists and nobody is truly saved? This is the Mystery Babylon. You need to be on full guard. This is also a method used to deceive the very elect! The end times are here right now and the great apostasy is before your very eyes to behold. Your church is fully involved with apostasy and dragging you along to the fires of hell. Escape now!

December 22

Few have the courage to stand for truth. Most churchgoers are too busy sitting in the pew or kneeling before their pastor to be bothered to contend for the faith one delivered to the saints. No wonder the Bible says the fearful shall not enter heaven. These cowards will not obey the commands of Jesus. They won't save the lost and they do not "seek" the lost.

December 23

Church is for sinners? Don't kid yourself. The apostles would never invite unrepentant sinners into their company to fellowship with them, but your pastor will not hesitate to run a newspaper advertisement inviting pagans to come to his church to fellowship with you. Times have certainly changed. If you challenge your pastor about this Biblical principal you will be punished. The Bible says Jesus was despised and rejected by men Isaiah 53:3. Christians think only pagans and unbelievers can do that, but Christians do it ever worse! If you try to preach Jesus' own Words in your church the church members and the pastor will eventually say, *"Away with him. We will not have this!"* Go ahead and say the unpopular Words, warnings and commands of Jesus and see this rejection excommunicate you from their midst. It's happening in many churches; get rid of fundamental Bible believing Christians! Away with them and their Jesus! John 11:48, 19-6-15.

December 24

To become like Jesus is to go to church each week and listen to a pastor's sermon. Really? Does the Bible say or imply this? Are you being duped or what? Didn't Jesus walk in public places proclaiming the gospel? Or did he just go to church each week like you do? Are you really like Jesus or are you following a *different* Jesus? Is this what the Father told you to do to do His will? Matthew 7:21. What you do may be at odds with God's Will. What do you do anyway for God each day?

December 25

The Words of Jesus are unimportant, has no special significance and are to be ignored and not performed. What is really important is to just believe in Jesus. Believe you are saved. Believe your pastor's sermons and all will be well with you. Is this the prevailing results seen in your church? Who is obeying Jesus in your church? Show me their good works. Who is leaving gospel tracts around town? Who is teaching about apostasy in the church? Who is obeying Jesus' Words? You get the idea.

December 26

"A new Commandment I give you. Go to church each week." Jesus never said that. Don't you think if it were so important he would have? Think! Think! Jesus never said, *"Go to church."*

December 27

Test yourself to see if you are in the faith. II Corinthians 13:15. Visit JamesRussellPublishing.com and Take The Test. It's free. It is a simple multiple choise test. If you pass you are one of the blessed on your way to Heaven. If you fail, you will likely go to Hell. Curious? Take The Test.

December 28

Saint James has a message for you. Read: James 1:22. Now do what he says to do. You need to be told your dead faith can not save you. Gospel of James is not taught in the pulpit. Pators are silent. They have essentially taken scizzors and snipped out this gospel from your eyes and ears.

December 29

Are you living for self or living for God? If you are living for God then list what you did for God each day last week? Did you share the gospel to how many people last week? Did you leave any gospel literature anywhere so people could find and read it? Who are you really living for?

December 30

Your pastor tells you that you are saved. He loves to quote John 3:16 but Saint John in verse 3:26 says... *"but he who does not obey the Son will not see life, but the wrath of God abides upon him."* That's you! You got to obey Jesus, not your pastor. Get it? Does it make sense now?

December 31

Then there are believer conventions. What good comes out of these great assemblies? Nothing! The lost do not get saved before, during or after the convention ends. Nobody is inspired to go out and save the lost. After all the singing, preaching and cheering the pastors are leaving with pockets stashed with cash and the flock craving for more emotional uplifting then go back to their churches to tell of the wonderful time they had. The hopelessly lost are abandoned never to hear the gospel. This is the unfruitful works believer conventions produce.

Are people being spiritually affected by your daily life? If people are not receiving the gospel message by your daily activity you must seriously examine where or not you are actually in the faith. Is your fruit basket empty? You may not even be born-again. Many churchgoers are not born-again, but they are being told and assured that they are by pastors intent on making them happy.

JUDGMENT DAY

This day will come like a thief in the night and it will be utterly useless to say you are a church member. You will be judged by the Word of God and what you did with it while on Earth. When the books are opened evidence will be demanded. Yes, evidence. Evidence of fruit. You will be judged not how you spoke or what you professed or how many times you went to church. You will be judged on how you lived for God and what you did for Him and how you obeyed Him and did His will. Don't let a pastor deceive you that you will not see Judgment. Jesus said you will be judged! Get ready for that day will come. Fear it now. Consider your ways. Examine yourself. Fear the Lord. Do what He says to do.

I hope this book has awakened you from your slumber and that you too become a soldier of Jesus Christ of Nazareth to share the gospel of the Bible, expose apostasy, contend for the faith, share the gospel to the lost and be obedient to the Lord, not to any man. - *James Russell*

Death Notices

> Want to find a good church? Create your own; meeting in your own home just like the New Testament church did! Let the people associate for <u>true fellowship</u>. Use the KJV Bible and do what the Early Church did. Help each other, be wise who is invited and use discipline when needed to get the bums out who will not repent. <u>Don't let a pastor become an absolute authority</u> or become a focal point. That means no routine and expected sermons or storytelling. <u>Teach the whole counsel of God and go share the gospel to save the lost and refrain from "recruiting" church membership just to grow your church and keep the church groups small so everyone can know each other</u>. Don't build or purchase or rent any church building! If the church grows, create more home meeting places. Be leery of any entertainment.
>
> Don't be like apostate churches in any way. Be Biblical as much as possible. Baptize in public places like Jesus did. Never incorporate or file for tax-exempt status, so your church remains under Jesus' control. Do not pay salaries or wages. Do not invest or own property in the church name and don't let pastors own or control the church. If you can't control it, break up the church. If it fails, just start over if need be. <u>Do what Jesus commands</u> and you will now have a true church that will bear much good fruit!

YOUR BRAIN HURT YET?

It should hurt! After all the false indoctrination and the indignant anger of being deceived your brain should be overwhelmed by now. It will take time, a lot of time, to get a handle on how pastors deceive people. Just keep on keeping on contending for the faith once delivered to the saints. Expose the false prophets! This is your calling! We all must contend.

OR BE LEFT BEHIND

The Bible says to come to the Lord while you can as He will not strive with you for long. This is your chance to get right with God and rededicate yourself to serving Him, not your church and not your pastor. Serve Him by doing His will. It's that simple. Do what He told you to do in His Bible. Come early or be left behind in your church!

STOP PAYING TITHES

Stop paying tithes to pastors that are not contending for the faith and are not teaching the believers how to go save the lost <u>on a daily basis</u>. Supporting such pastors that disobey the Lord and win not souls <u>makes you a participant of his evil works</u>. You are supporting that unfruitful work of darkness.

What should you do? <u>Start your own ministry and take your tithe and offering money and invest it into gospel literature that will save the lost for Christ</u>. Now you will obey the Lord and be accountable. Your reward in heaven is assured. Giving money to your church will not be credited.

Instruction & Training

NOTICE THE FLOWERS

Your pastor adorns himself with flowers in his sanctuary inside his church building. These are not gifts to God, they are planted on purpose to impress upon your mind the special purpose the pastor has in your life. He walks and preaches among the flowers to impress you for it certainly does not impress God one bit. None of this is Biblical whatsoever for even Jesus did not walk and preach in a garden setting to glorify his image before man, but pastor's do! Open you eyes and you will see more gimmicks, always more gimmicks to gain your loyalty and trust. Beware!

Dear author of this book, my pastor would never deceive anyone as you say. He is the most honorable man I know... oops, the second most honorable man beside Jesus, but what Jesus? Duh, let me start over.

WE WON'T GO!

There are churches that do obey the Bible almost to a "T" but there you will find one missing command every church refuses to do. These church members still will not go out on their own to reach the lost. They won't obey the Lord's desire to save that which is lost. None carry gospel tracts with them and they will not leave them wherever they go. Satan loves religion, just don't go save the lost! That's his plan. Cities should be plastered with tracts, but Christians have stolen salvation for themselves not to share it. Matt. 24:24. And they are given strong delusion to believe a lie so they all might be damned! 2 Thes. 2:11.

LORD, FIND SOMEBODY ELSE TO DO YOUR DIRTY WORK! AS FOR ME AND MY HOUSE... <u>WE SHALL SERVE OUR PASTOR</u>!

They avoid sharing the gospel at all costs and they refuse to even leave gospel tracts around town in their daily travels. They have no interest to obey Jesus.

THOU SHALT <u>NOT</u>
Disobey your pastor! It is better for you to go to church each week than to waste your precious time to save the lost for Christ. ObeyYourPastorNotJesus.com!

RESOURCES

This is your chance to learn more about the great apostate Christian religions and help yourself escape from their iron clad grasp. It is important for you to flee from their churches! And, when you have learned about this great falling away do your Christian duty to warn others so they too may escape! Contact these resources.

Chick Publications
P.O. Box 3500
Ontario, CA 91761-1019
Chick.com

Foundation Magazine
Fundamental Evangelistic Assoc.
1476 W. Herndon Ave., Suite 104
Fresno, CA 93711
Feasite.org

The Testimony of Truth
People of the Living God
366 Cove Creek Road
McMinnville, TN 37110-9512
PeopleOfTheLivingGod.org

Moments With The Book
PO Box 322
Bedford, PA 15522
MWTB.org

JamesRussellPublishing.com

Note: If there are any glaring errors in this book we will post corrections on our Web site.

BOOKS TO READ

Apostasy From The Bible, John Owen, ISBN 0- 85151-609-2.

The Great Dream - The Great and Final Apostasy of Christendom Described, ISBN 981-04-1958-9.

The Lost gospel of John by James Russell, ISBN 9780916367572.

The Lost gospel of James by James Russell, ISBN 9780916367725.

Lie of the Ages by Todd Tomasella, ISBN 1-4259-7278-0.

More books and updated listings:
Visit: JamesRussellPublishing.com

THE END

Book Catalog

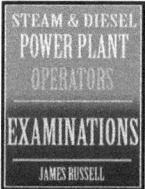

STEAM & DIESEL POWER PLANT OPERATORS EXAMINATIONS
ISBN-10: 0-916367-08-8 ISBN-13: 978-0-916367- 08-4
117 pp., 8x11, illustrated, $34.95 Over 1,400 multiple-choice test questions & answers (with explanations) helps stationary engineer power plant operators pass steam boiler licensing and pre-employment exams. This book has the answers to the exams!

TRAP SHOOTING SECRETS
ISBN-10: 0-916367-09-6 ISBN-13: 978-0-916367- 09-1
18-3 pp., 8x11, 85 illustrations, $34.95. There has never been a book like this, ever! *TSS* is like having a shooting coach telling you precisely what to do to hit the targets. It is the first book ever to be endorsed by professional trap shooters!

PRECISION SHOOTING - THE TRAPSHOOTER'S BIBLE
ISBN-10: 0-916367-10-X ISBN-13: 978-0-916367-10-7
230 pp., 8x11, 145 illustrations, $34.95. The *only* trap shooting book with ATA & Olympic Double-Trap technical instructions. The *only* professional advanced-level trapshooting book in the world. Has hundreds of answers to competition shooting questions in great detail to help you understand precisely what professional shooters know.

SCREEN & STAGE MARKETING SECRETS
ISBN-10: 0-916367-11-8 ISBN-13: 978-0-916367-11-4
177 pp., 8x11, 60 illustrations $34.95. The only book specifically written for writers to sell television and feature film movie screenplays and theatrical stage plays to literary agents and production companies. Many books explain how to write scripts, but this one tells how to get them sold! Insider industry secrets of marketing scritps are revealed.

INTERNET ADDRESS BOOK WITH COMPUTER BACK UP FILES
ISBN-10: 0-916367-12-6 ISBN-13: 978-0-916367- 12-1
116 pp., 8x11, $19.95 Never lose another important password, ID number, e-mail or Internet contact. Log them here in this book. Also, enter your computer data files so you can recover from computer failure, theft, fire, flood, or just making a file deletion error.

AN EVENING OF COMEDY SKITS – 11 TEN MINUTE THEATRICAL PLAYS
ISBN-10: 0-916367-32-0 ISBN-13: 978-0-916367-32-9
117 pp., 8x11, $34.95. A collection of 11 ten minute comedy sketches. Plays are low budget with common household props and focusing on the funny relationships between men and women. Two parodies included of two TV shows: "Cops" and "The Dating Game. Suitable for general audiences.

James Russell Publishing.com

STAGE PLAY – A COMEDY THEATRICAL PLAY
ISBN-10: 0-916367-34-7   ISBN-13: 978-0-916367- 34-3
132 pp., 8x11, $12.95 Two women must get married at all cost and they pick two goofy actors using every trick in the book to get the "I do". A fast-pace, low-budget, full-length comedy play focusing on the courtship ritual. No harsh offensive dialog. Common household props. Strong emotional acting.

TRUE BUMS - A COMEDY SCREENPLAY
ISBN-10: 0-916367-26-6   ISBN-13: 978-0-916367-26-8
118 pp., 8x11, $12.95. Three movie executives burned out on life escape the good life of Hollywood to become bobos on a California railroad. Here they discover other rich men doing the same, living the high-life in lavish Disneyland-like fantasy whistle stops, until the wives find out, steal a freight train and the great train chase is on. The bums must save Christmas at all costs from the wives who are determined to capture and return them home, forever!

REVENGE OF THE GRANNIES - A COMEDY SCREENPLAY
ISBN-10: 0-916367-25-8   ISBN-13: 978-0-916367-25-1
124 pp., 8x11, $12.95 Rich grandmothers fed up with crime and a corrupt mayor form a military assault team, MEBOM, to wage full-scale war against the city of Lost Angus street gangs and city hall. Military fireworks and destruction is severe, though nobody is killed in this comedy screenplay. Grandma is the hero!

WALKING WITH THE LORD A CHRISTIAN DEVOTIONAL – DAILY INSPIRATIONAL & WITNESSING INSTRUCTIONS
ISBN-10: 0-916367-19-3   ISBN-13: 978-0-916367-19-0
140 pp., 8x11, $12.95. A powerful daily devotional focusing on what a believer can do for the Lord with hundreds of instructions on how to prepare for God's service. Become a positive and effective witnesses to the Lord. Written for those who believe the Bible to bear good fruit.

HOW TO CHANGE THE OIL IN YOUR TWIN CAM HARLEY-DAVIDSON MOTORCYCLE
ISBN-10: 0-916367-75-6   ISBN-13: 978-0-916367-75-6
144 pp., 5.5x8.5, $34.95 A guide on how to change the three oil compartments on the motorcycle. Also replacing the air filter and spark plugs with valuable engine longevity advice. Written for the rider who wants to learn how to do it himself. This book makes it easy to learn with 80 photographs and highly detailed step-by-step instructions.

THE OATMAN ARIZONA HOLY LAND TOUR
ISBN-10: 0-916367-17-7   ISBN-13: 978-0-916367-17-6
104 pp., 5.5x8.5, 60 photographs, $19.95 A Self-guided 60 mile automobile and motorcycle tour of Arizona rock formations resembling Biblical scenes near Oatman, Arizona. A new tourist attraction near Laughlin, Nevada. The tour is on Route 66 and entirely accessible by paved roads. No other tourist attraction in the USA has more Biblical rock formations than in Oatman, Arizona. The tour is on old Route 66.

Book Catalog

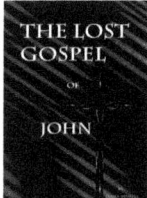

THE LOST GOSPEL OF JOHN
ISBN-13: 978-0-916367-57-2

306 pp., 6.x9 $24.95 Discover a different, more powerful and entertaining Jesus you never knew existed. Experience strange and unusual parables, incredibly wild miracles, intense wisdom and fabulous sermons that will lift you to heavenly realms. Relive John's eye-witness commentaries never before published until now. A novel that will educate and enlighten with a very serious message.

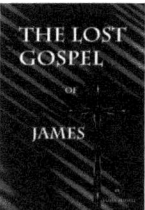

THE LOST GOSPEL OF JAMES
ISBN-13: 978-0-916367-59-6

320 pp., 6x9 $24.95 A continuation of *The Lost Gospel of John* this book advances the series with Saint James version of the gospel. A bonus feature of gospels from unknown saints of old are now included. James exposes apostate teachers and warns of the dangers of being too productive for the Lord and takes you to see the beauty of heaven, the fires and pains of hell and whisks you away to exciting pagan festivals around the world.

PROFESSIONAL TARGET SHOOTER'S DIARY & JOURNAL
ISBN-13: 978-0-916367-60-2

236 pp., 6x9 $24.95 A *combined* diary and journal specific to the target shooting sports to log competitive event pre-conditions to jog the memory of unfavorable environments, to record score, conditions, ammo, equipment modifications, etc. There are 108 shooting club (or event) listings, so there is ample room for attending and logging entries into many competitive events and practice sessions. Never be taken by surprise again forgetting what you should have remembered.

PROFESSIONAL SPORTSMAN'S EXPENSE LOG BOOK
ISBN-13: 978-0-916367-61-9

230 pp., 6x9 $24.95 Take a full tax deduction on all your sporting equipment! That's right, you can. This is the book that gets you started into the professional arena even if you are still in training and not a professional. So easy to begin you can start deducting the moment you buy the book, including practice and competitive event fees, gasoline, clothing, and dozens more deductions. It's like getting a huge pay raise! And there are no license or business fees whatsoever. Save money now!

APOSTASY DEVOTIONAL BOOK
ISBN-13: 978-0-916367-62-6

160 pp., 6x9 $24.95 This is the first published daily Christian devotional book giving remarkable insight every day of the year exposing false shepherd pastors ruling in the church today. You will learn the secrets pastors use to control and manipulate their congregations and peel back the disguise deceiving millions of churchgoers. Discover how pastors get believers to obey them... yet disobey Jesus and do it without being caught. You're in for one wild ride. Get the Biblical truth teaching you how to escape the great falling away. Stop being duped! Get the book.

James Russell Publishing.com

BOOK ORDER FORM

QUANTITY   TITLE   RETAIL PRICE
___Steam & Diesel Power Plant Examinations $34.95
___Trap Shooting Secrets $34.95
___Precision Shooting - The Trapshooters Bible $34.95
___Screen & Stage Marketing Secrets $34.95
___Internet Address Book $12.95
___An Evening of Comedy Skits $34.95
___Walking With The Lord Christian Devotional $12.95
___True Bums $12.95
___Revenge of the Grannies $12.95
___Stage Play $12.95
___How to Change the Oil in Your Twin Cam Harley-Davidson Motorcycle - $34.95
___The Oatman Arizona Holy Land Tour $19.95
___The Lost Gospel of John $24.95
___The Lost Gospel of James $24.95
___ Professional Target Shooter's Diary & Journal $24.95
___ Professional Sportsman's Expense Log Book $24.95
___ Apostasy Devotional Book $24.95

Shipping: $6 first book. Add $2 for each additional book. _____
Nevada business: Sales/Use Tax resale number # _____
TOTAL: Shipping Charge and Purchase Price of Books $ _____
Send order and payment to the mailing address listed on our Web site.

BOOKSTORES: PLEASE PURCHASE OUR BOOKS FROM OUR WHOLESALERS
For Print on Demand books contact Lightning Source listed here.
Baker & Taylor: www.btol.com Phone 908-218-3950
Ingram: www.ingrambookgroup.com Phone 800-937-8000
Lightning Source USA www.lightningsource.com Phone 615-213-5815
Brodart Company: www.brodart.com Phone 800-233-8467
Spring Arbor also wholesales our Christian books. Phone 800-395-4340

James Russell, SAN 295-852X. Web site: JamesRussellPublishing.com
E-mail: Jrpub2002@yahoo.com